GASPARD TALMASSE

ALICE ON THE RUN

ONE CHILD'S JOURNEY THROUGH THE RWANDAN CIVIL WAR

Life Drawn by Humanoids

GASPARD TALMASSE

ALICE ON THE RUN

ONE CHILD'S JOURNEY THROUGH THE RWANDAN CIVIL WAR

Gaspard Talmasse
Writer & Artist

Nanette McGuinness
Translator

Jonathan Stevenson
Letterer

Jonathan Stevenson
English-Language Edition Editor

Vincent Henry
Original Edition Editor

Sandy Tanaka
Designer

Jerry Frissen
Senior Art Director

Mark Waid
Publisher

Rights and Licensing - licensing@humanoids.com
Press and Social Media - pr@humanoids.com

ALICE ON THE RUN: ONE CHILD'S JOURNEY THROUGH THE RWANDAN CIVIL WAR. First Printing. This book is a publication of Humanoids, Inc. 8033 Sunset Blvd. #628, Los Angeles, CA 90046.

Library of Congress Control Number: 2022933313

Life Drawn is an imprint of Humanoids, Inc.

Printed in Latvia.

THROUGH ALICE'S EYES

by Jean-Hervé Bradol, Doctors Without Borders

One child's story cannot sum up all of the many atrocities that Rwandans were victims of during the 1990s. Alice tells us her own story: how she crossed the Democratic Republic of Congo on foot for over 1200 miles, from east to west. Of the groups of fugitives, three out of four were women and children. Among them were also militiamen and soldiers who, before losing the war and leaving Rwanda in 1994, had taken part in the genocide against their Tutsi compatriots. The number of victims is estimated at around 800,000. The winners of the Rwandan civil war and their Congolese allies pursued these Rwandan refugees who had settled in the Democratic Republic of Congo, tracking them and using humanitarian aid to trap them. When they found the refugees, they gave them no quarter. Children—no matter their age—pregnant women, the elderly: everyone was killed. That is why despite exhaustion, hunger, illness, wild animals, and terror, some of the refugees kept walking. Alice survived to tell us about all of it.

We know this story because among those who fled—as is the case with all types of people who are victims of atrocities in the African Great Lakes region—were members of Médecins Sans Frontières (Doctors Without Borders). A huge thank you to Alice and Gaspard for their sensitivity and accuracy in telling us their version of this story we share with you.

Ever since gaining its independence, Rwanda had been governed by Hutus (typically farmers) to the detriment of Tutsis (primarily herders). Starting in 1990, a civil war raged between rebels from the Rwandan Patriotic Front (RPF)—consisting of Tutsis exiled in Uganda and led by Paul Kagame—and the Rwandan Armed Forces (FAR).

On April 7, 1994, in Rwanda, a genocide began that killed roughly 800,000 people, mostly Tutsis. The night before, a plane carrying the Rwandan and Burundi presidents, Juvénal Habyrimana and Cyprien Ntaryamira, was destroyed by a missile of unknown origin.

During the night following the attack, many moderate Hutu political figures were assassinated, as well as ten Belgian peacekeepers. When the extremist Hutu militias—often subsumed under the name of the strongest of them, Interahamwe—carried out the first massacres, the UN decided to reduce its intervention force from 2,500 to 250. Without significant international action, the violence multiplied.

The advance of the RPF troops is what actually put an end to the genocide: the fall of Kigali on July 4, 1994 and gaining control of the majority of the country on July 17, 1994. Fleeing the RPF's advance, a million Hutus crossed the Zairian border (today's Democratic Republic of Congo). Among them were many who had taken part in the genocide—FAR soldiers with all their weapons—but also civilians, including children, who were caught in the crossfire.

Jean-Hervé Bradol is a physician who specializes in tropical medicine, emergency medicine, and epidemiology, Jean-Hervé Bradol went on his first mission with MSF in 1989, undertaking long assignments in Uganda, Somalia, and Thailand. He is the author of numerous publications, including Medical Innovations In Humanitarian Situations *(CreateSpace, 2011) and* Humanitarian Aid, Genocide, And Mass Killings: The Rwandan Experience 1982-97 *(Manchester University Press, 2017).*

April 1994

RWANDA - NEAR GITARAMA

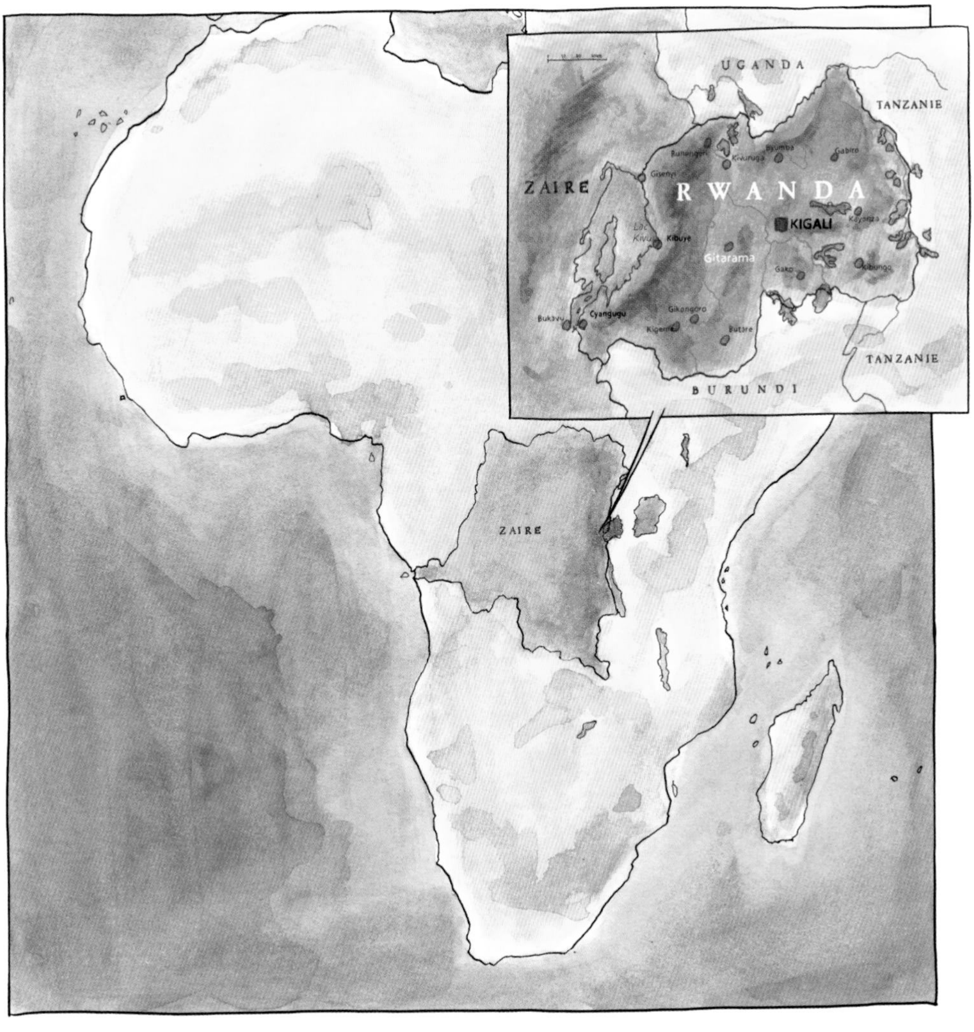

UGANDA
TANZANIE
ZAIRE
RWANDA
KIGALI
Gitarama
TANZANIE
BURUNDI
ZAIRE

LATE APRIL 1994. RWANDA, NOT FAR FROM GITARAMA.

MY NAME IS ALICE.

I WAS FIVE THEN.
MY LITTLE SISTERS, THE TWINS...
...ADELINE AND ALINE...
...WERE THREE.

* RWANDAN PATRIOTIC FRONT.

ONE DAY, I WENT WITH MY SISTERS AND MY UNCLE (WHO WAS MY AGE) TO GO PLAY WITH OUR COUSINS, AS USUAL.

I CAN HEAR SOMETHING. IT SOUNDS LIKE PEOPLE.

WHEN WE GOT TO THE MAIN ROAD, WE SAW THEM.
WHAT'S GOING ON?

SOME MEN WERE HITTING ANOTHER MAN WITH CLUBS.

BOOM

HE WAS LYING ON THE GROUND...

POUM

*INYENZI ("COCKROACHES"): NAME GIVEN TO THE TUTSIS.

AFTER THAT,
THINGS CHANGED.

WE COULDN'T GO
OUT TO PLAY ANYMORE.
ALICE, COME BACK!

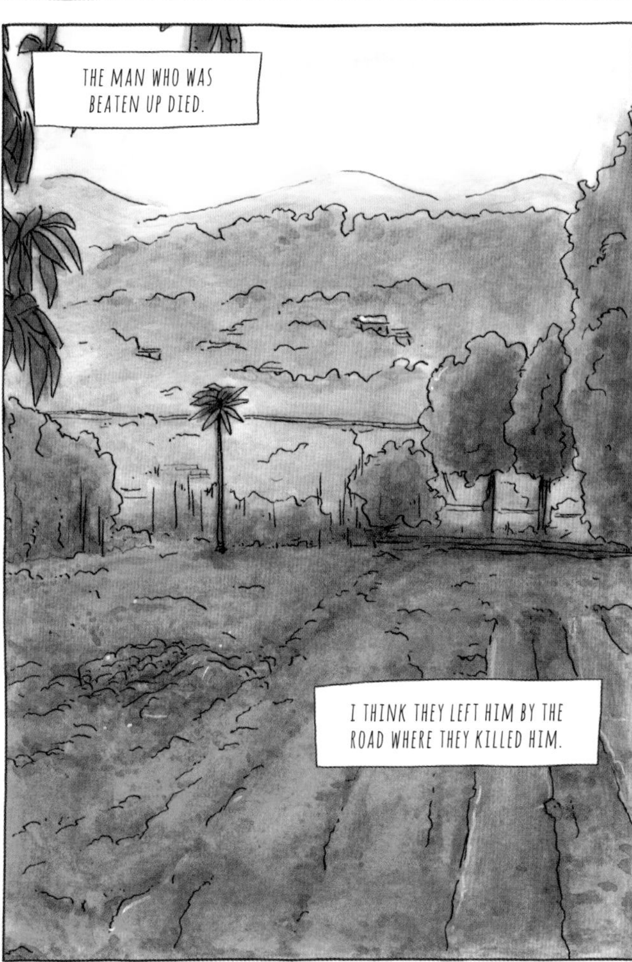
THE MAN WHO WAS
BEATEN UP DIED.
I THINK THEY LEFT HIM BY THE
ROAD WHERE THEY KILLED HIM.

I NEVER WENT TO
THAT PLACE AGAIN.

LATE MAY 1994.
I REMEMBER ONE MORNING...

IT WAS ABOUT A MONTH LATER...

WE WERE WOKEN UP BY NOISES OUTSIDE.

OUR PARENTS WENT OUT TO LOOK.

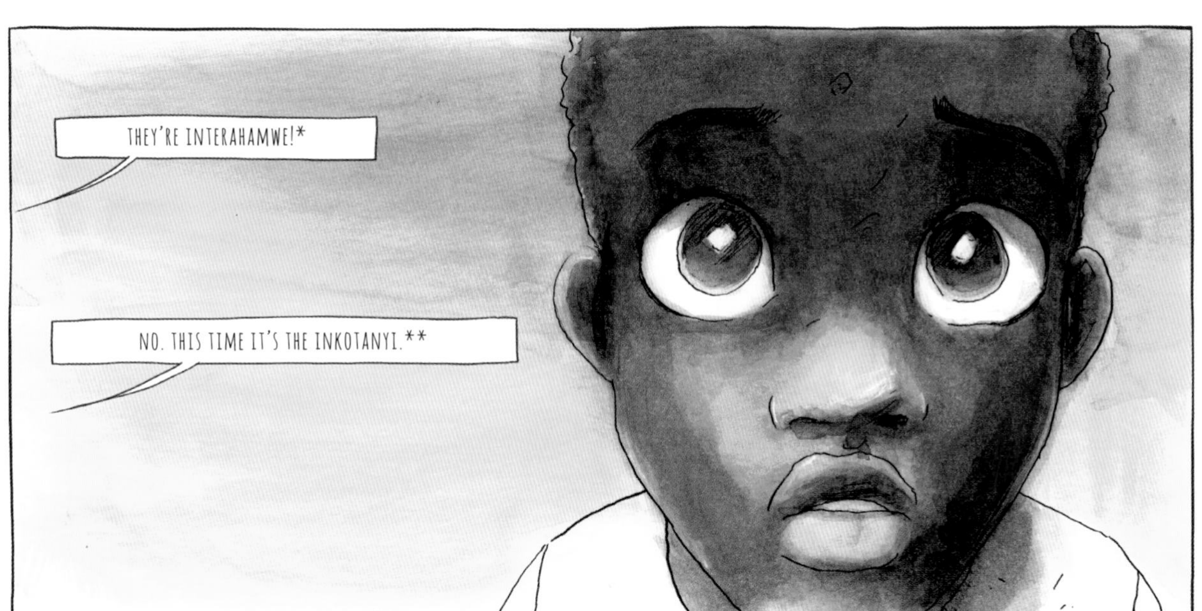

DO YOU THINK THEY'LL COME AFTER US?

IT LOOKS LIKE IT. ANYWAY, I DON'T WANT TO WAIT HERE TO FIND OUT.

WE HAVE TO LEAVE. RIGHT AWAY.

ON THE OTHER HILLSIDE, HOUSES WERE BURNING AND PEOPLE WERE SCREAMING.

*HUTU MILITIAMEN

**TUTSI SOLDIERS FROM THE RWANDAN PATRIOTIC FRONT.

AT FIRST, WE THOUGHT IT WAS A GAME...

OR THAT WE WERE GOING ON A TRIP TO VISIT SOMEONE.

THERE WERE SOLDIERS WITH US, TOO. I THINK THEY WERE RWANDAN MILITARY.

AFTER THAT, THINGS STARTED HAPPENING.

I FOUND MYSELF IN A TRUCK...

SITTING IN THE BACK
WITH MY SISTERS...

...ADELINE BEING HER
USUAL CRANKY SELF...

...ALINE IN HER OVERALLS...

...AND ROSE, A YOUNG GIRL MY
PARENTS HAD BROUGHT ALONG.

SHE'D COME TO STAY WITH US SEVERAL DAYS BEFORE.

ALICE, I'M GOING TO THE BATHROOM.

I DIDN'T UNDERSTAND THAT SHE HAD TO STAY HIDDEN.

WE HAVE TO MAKE SURE NOBODY'S COMING.

OKAY...

KEEP PLAYING HIDE AND SEEK
WHILE YOU'RE WAITING.

ADELINE'S IT!

ONE, SIX, THREE, NINE,
TWO, FIVE, TWELVE...

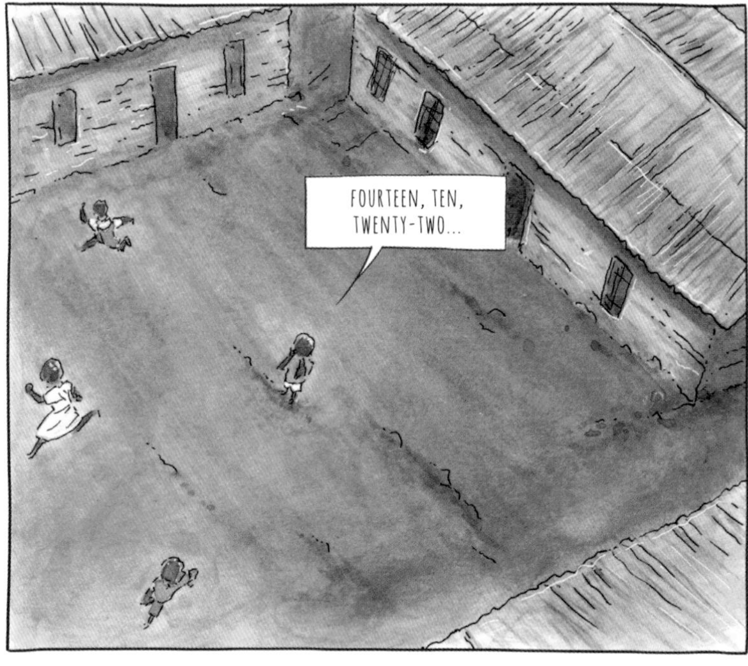
FOURTEEN, TEN,
TWENTY-TWO...

...ONE THOUSAND!

HEY THERE, KIDS.

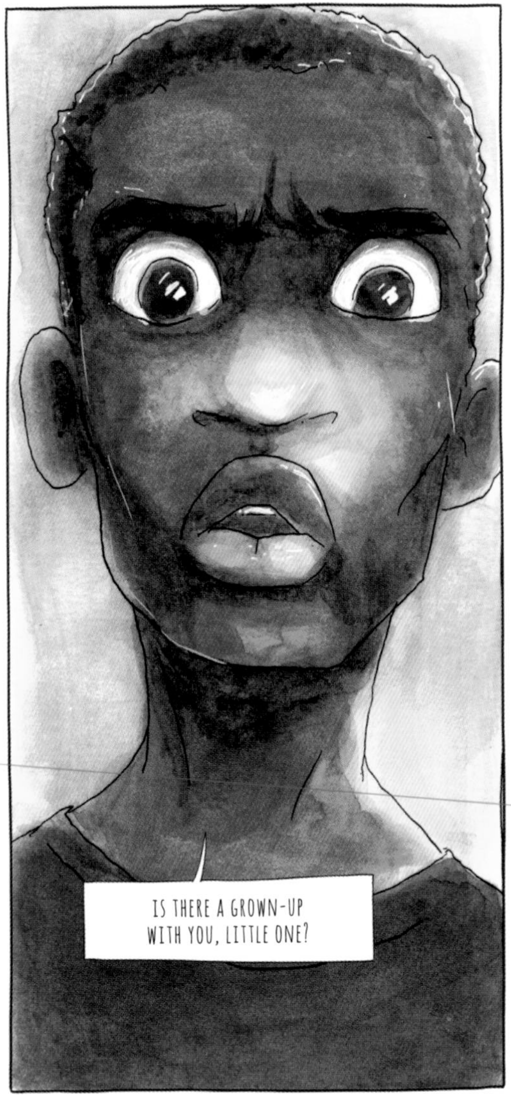
IS THERE A GROWN-UP
WITH YOU, LITTLE ONE?

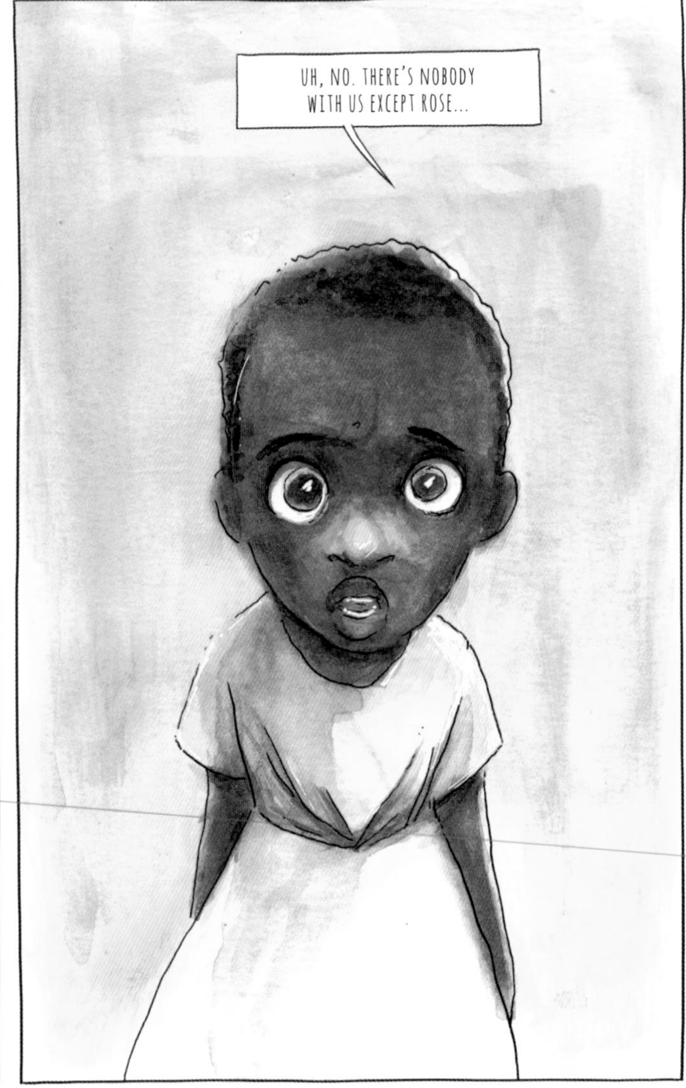
UH, NO. THERE'S NOBODY
WITH US EXCEPT ROSE...

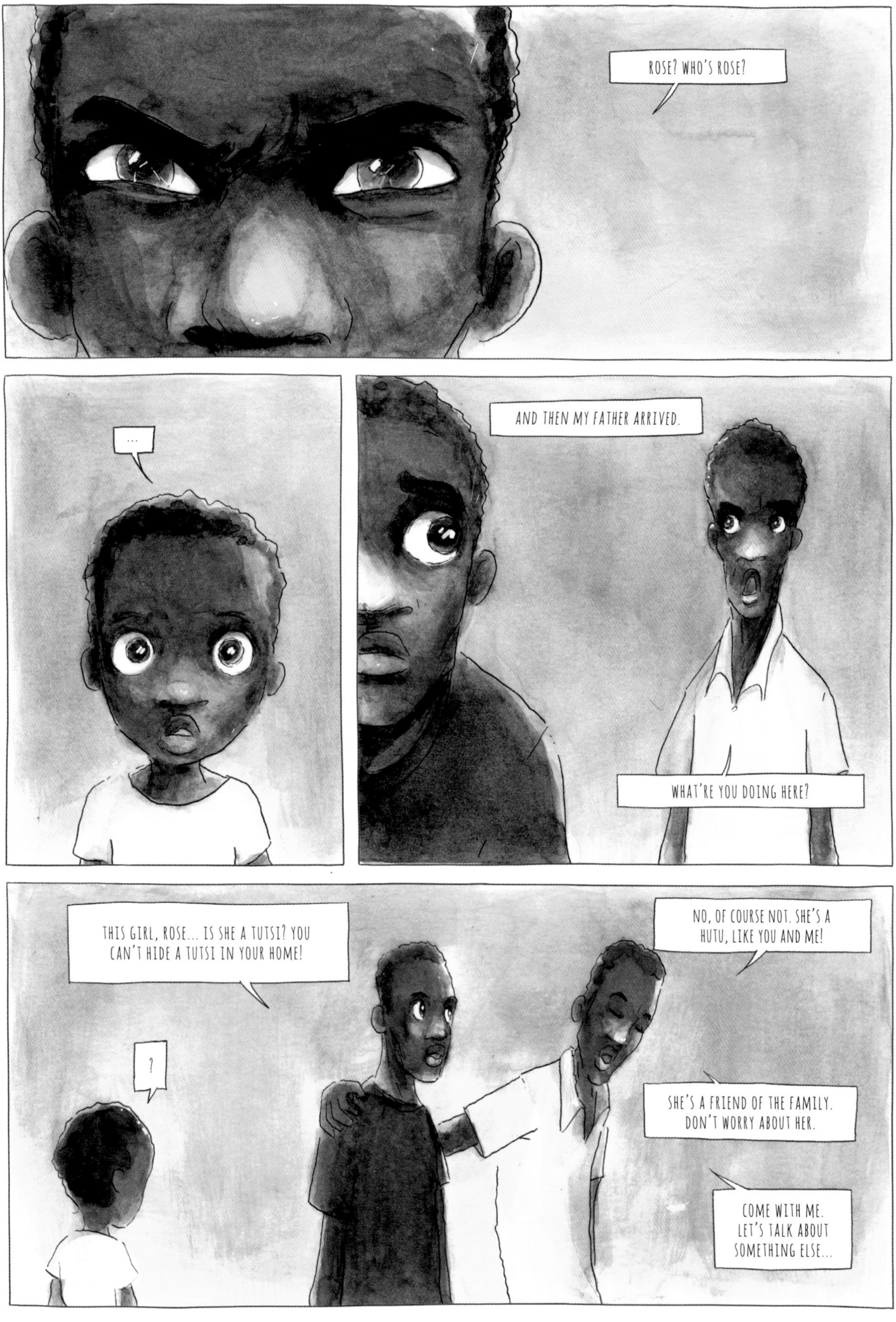

ROSE? WHO'S ROSE?

...

AND THEN MY FATHER ARRIVED.

WHAT'RE YOU DOING HERE?

THIS GIRL, ROSE... IS SHE A TUTSI? YOU CAN'T HIDE A TUTSI IN YOUR HOME!

NO, OF COURSE NOT. SHE'S A HUTU, LIKE YOU AND ME!

?

SHE'S A FRIEND OF THE FAMILY. DON'T WORRY ABOUT HER.

COME WITH ME. LET'S TALK ABOUT SOMETHING ELSE...

MID-JUNE 1994.
TWO WEEKS LATER, A WHITE TRUCK TOOK US TO KIBUYE, ON THE SHORE OF LAKE KIVU.

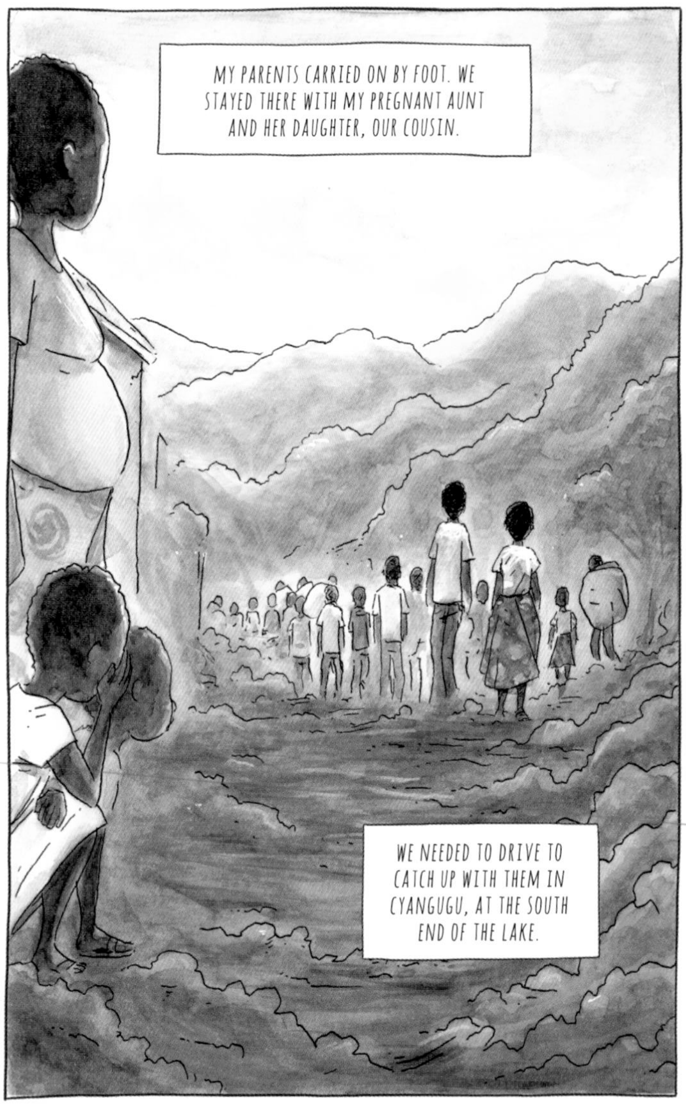
MY PARENTS CARRIED ON BY FOOT. WE STAYED THERE WITH MY PREGNANT AUNT AND HER DAUGHTER, OUR COUSIN.
WE NEEDED TO DRIVE TO CATCH UP WITH THEM IN CYANGUGU, AT THE SOUTH END OF THE LAKE.

BUT THE DRIVER NEVER CAME.

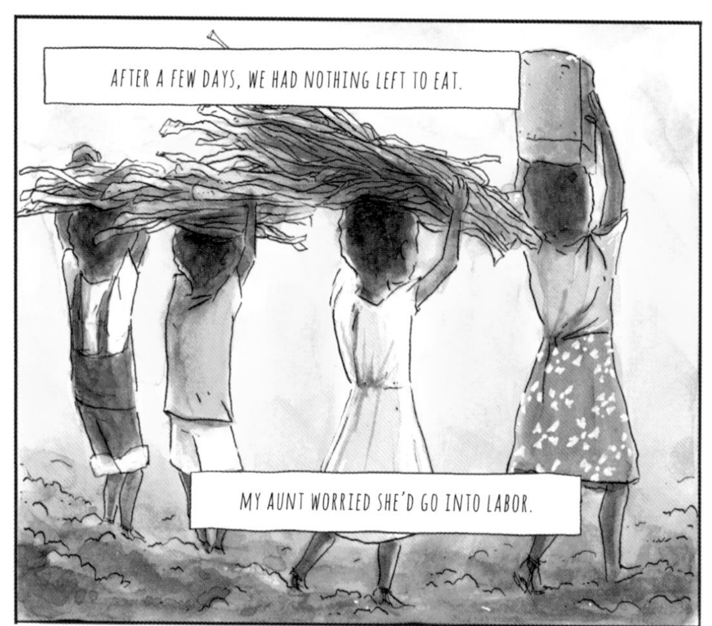
AFTER A FEW DAYS, WE HAD NOTHING LEFT TO EAT.
MY AUNT WORRIED SHE'D GO INTO LABOR.

SO IT WAS UP TO US KIDS TO GO FIND FOOD FOR EVERYONE, WOOD FOR THE FIRE, AND WATER.

WE WAITED A WEEK.

THEN MY FATHER CAME BACK TO FIND US, AND WE LEFT FOR CYANGUGU ON FOOT.

AT THE END OF JUNE 1994, AFTER WALKING FOR FIVE DAYS, WE REACHED A HOUSE THAT TOOK US IN. MY AUNT GAVE BIRTH RIGHT AWAY.
IT WAS A LITTLE BOY!
THE ADULTS LEFT TO TALK IN THE ROOM NEXT DOOR WHILE WE GOT TO KNOW THE BABY.
WE'RE SAFE NOW.
THIS WON'T LAST. THEY'LL BE COMING HERE AS SOON AS THEY CAN.
THEN WHAT? WE'LL HAVE TO GO TO ZAIRE?!
PROBABLY. BUT FOR NOW, LET'S JUST WAIT AND SEE WHAT HAPPENS.
WE'LL HAVE TO KEEP LISTENING TO THE RADIO.

August 1994

BUKAVU

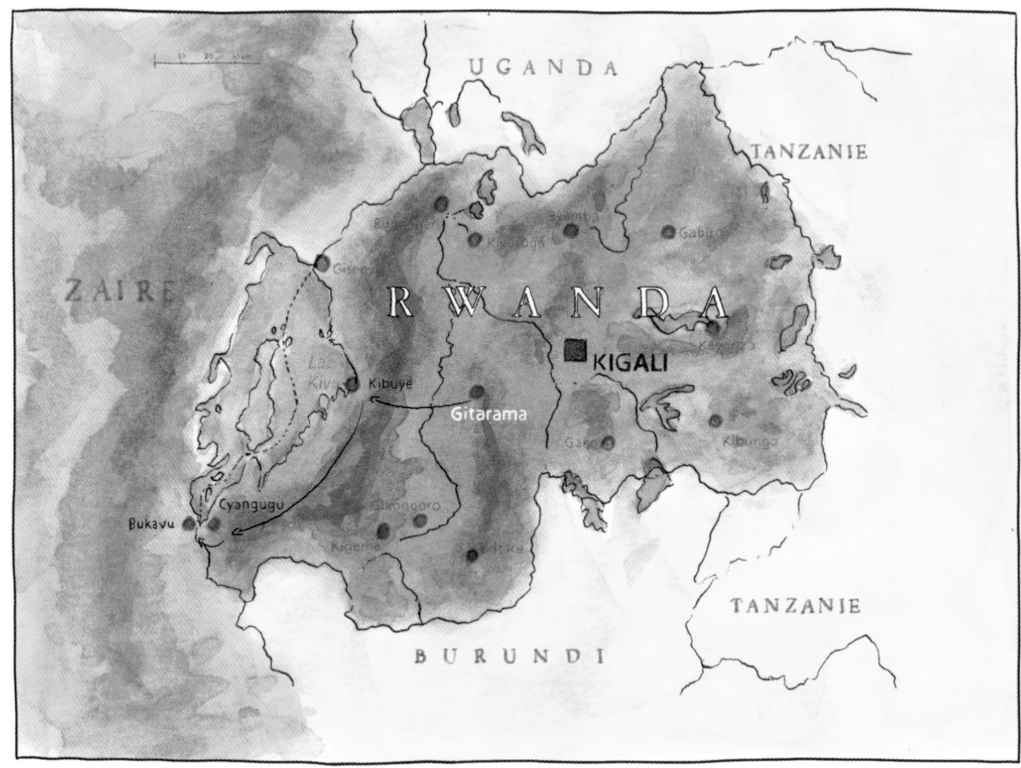

TIME PASSED. WE LEFT THE NICE FAMILY IN CYANGUGU, AND RWANDA ITSELF.
WE WENT TO BUKAVU, IN ZAIRE.

ROSE DIDN'T STAY WITH US IN BUKAVU. SHE WENT BACK TO RWANDA.

EVERYONE STARTED TO BUILD SHELTERS AND ARRANGE THEIR LIVES THERE.

I REMEMBER ONE NIGHT...

WE WERE SLEEPING OUTSIDE, AND IT STARTED RAINING.

STEAM WAS COMING OFF PEOPLE.

ADELINE, ALINE! ARE YOU ASLEEP?
WHAT'S GOING ON?

LOOK!

DADDY'S STEAMING!

LOOK, EVERYONE'S STEAMING.
HEE! HEE! THAT'S FUNNY!
YES, AND IT LOOKS LIKE THEY GOT WASHED WITH THEIR CLOTHES ON.

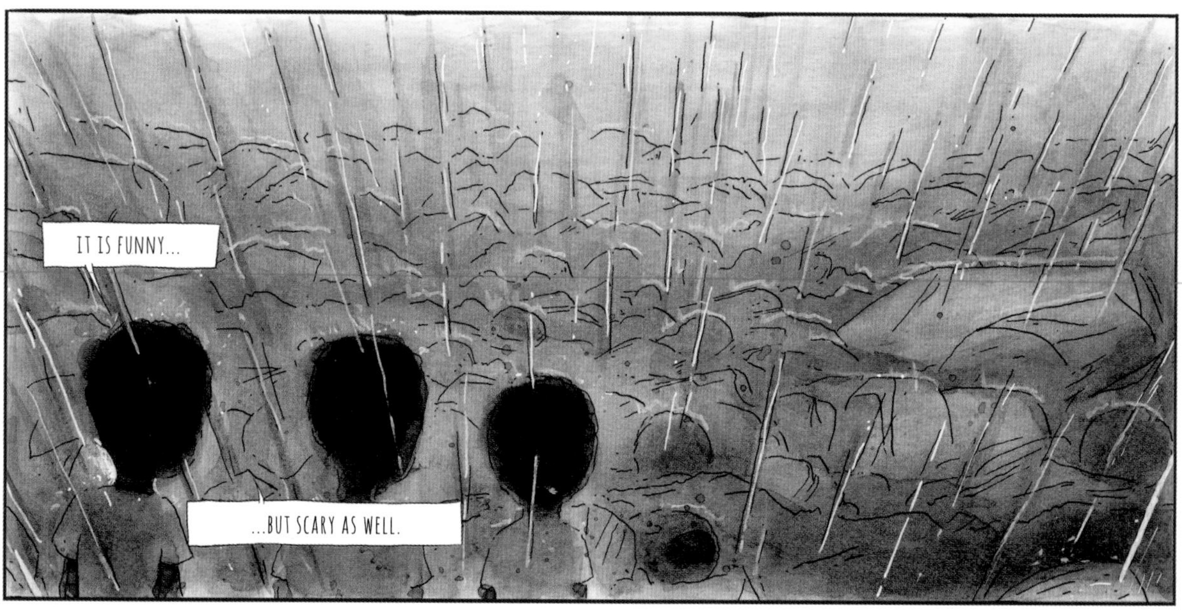
IT IS FUNNY...
...BUT SCARY AS WELL.

"WHAT'S WRONG WITH MAMA?"
"SHE HAS CHOLERA."

...
BECAUSE OF THE WATER.

IT'S **VERY** CONTAGIOUS. WE MUSTN'T GO NEAR HER!

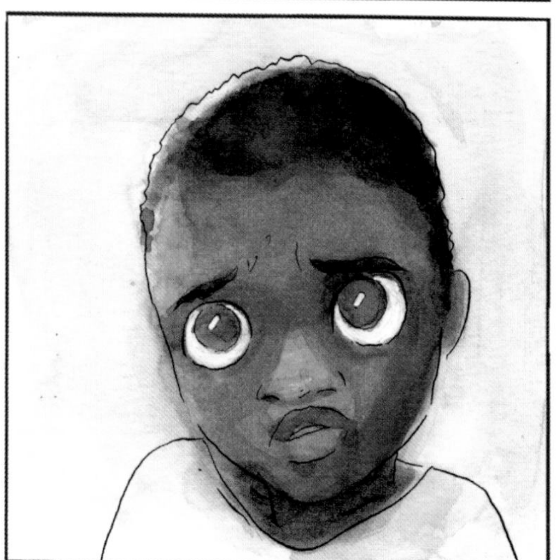

MANY PEOPLE GOT SICK.

ALICE?

YES?

MANY PEOPLE DIED.

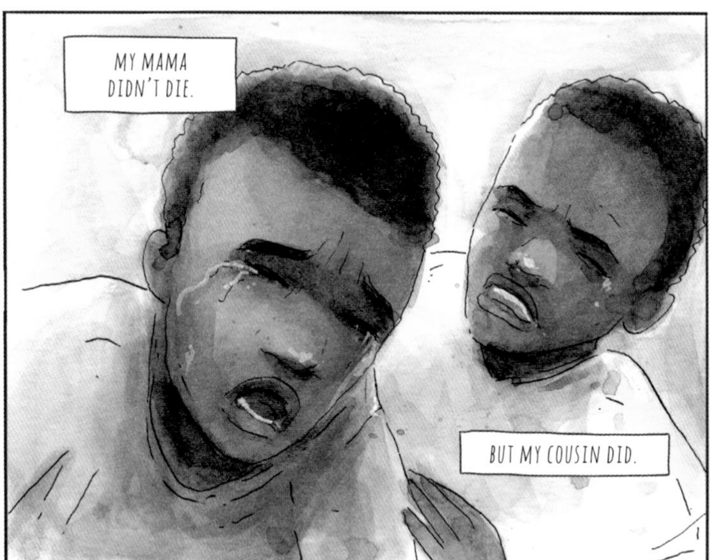
MY MAMA DIDN'T DIE.
BUT MY COUSIN DID.

MY AUNT WAS VERY SAD.
I DIDN'T UNDERSTAND WHAT DEATH WAS.

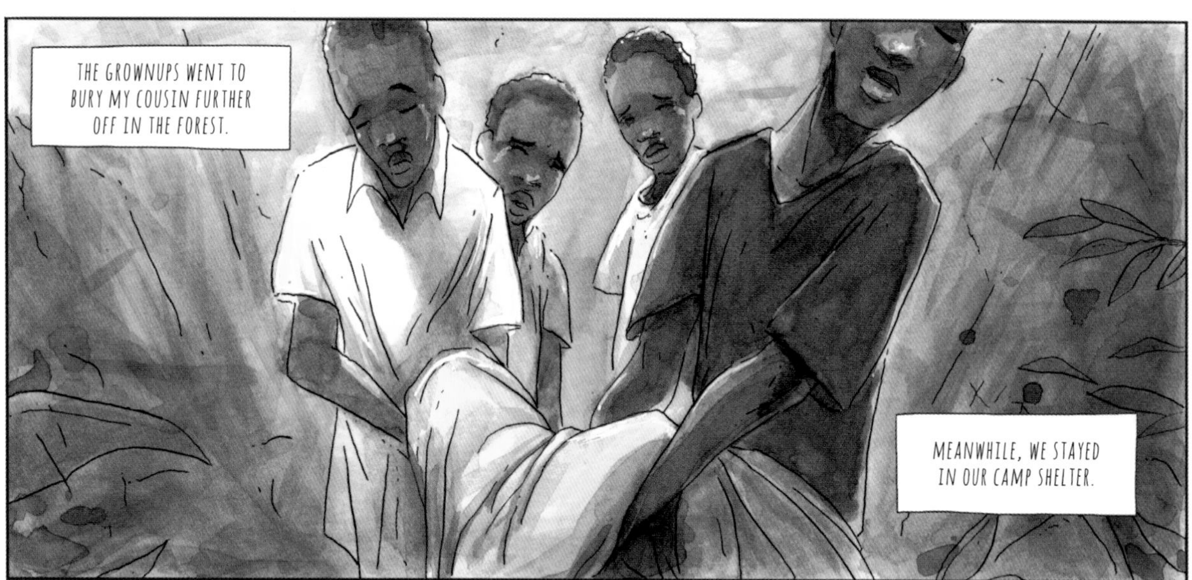
THE GROWNUPS WENT TO BURY MY COUSIN FURTHER OFF IN THE FOREST.
MEANWHILE, WE STAYED IN OUR CAMP SHELTER.

AFTERWARDS, MAMA CAME TO TALK TO ME.
ALICE, YOUR COUSIN HAS GONE TO MEET GOD.

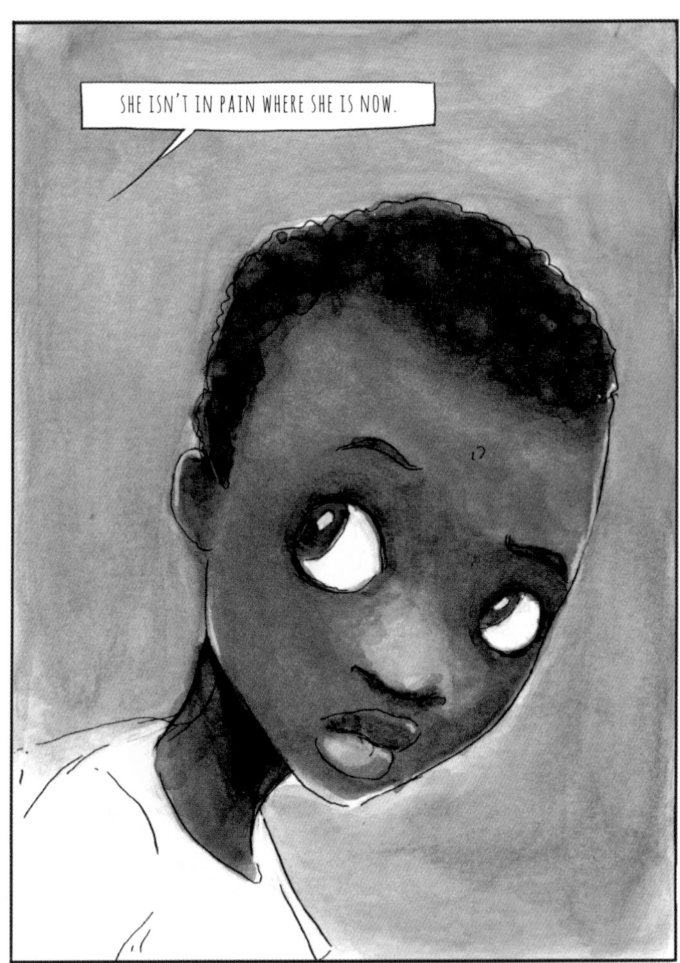
SHE ISN'T IN PAIN WHERE SHE IS NOW.

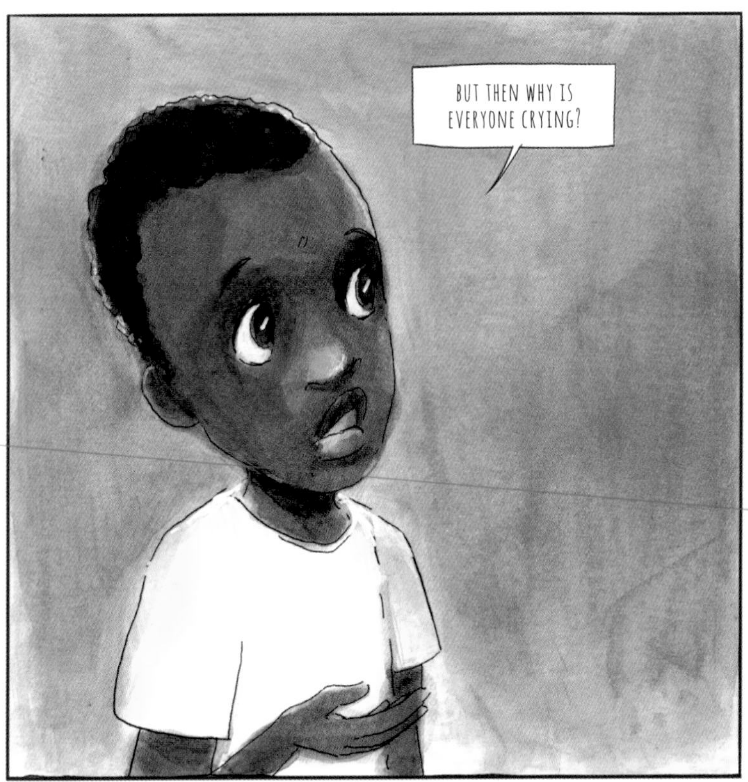
BUT THEN WHY IS EVERYONE CRYING?

...
WHY IS EVERYONE SAD?

WE BEGAN TO GET SOME HELP, AND LIFE BECAME MORE COMFORTABLE, EVEN IF WATER STILL CONTINUED TO BE A PROBLEM.

THE SCHOOLS OPENED, AND MAMA FOUND WORK AS A TEACHER.
MY FATHER LEFT FOR CENTRAL AFRICA TO CONTINUE HIS STUDIES. WE WERE SUPPOSED TO MEET LATER.

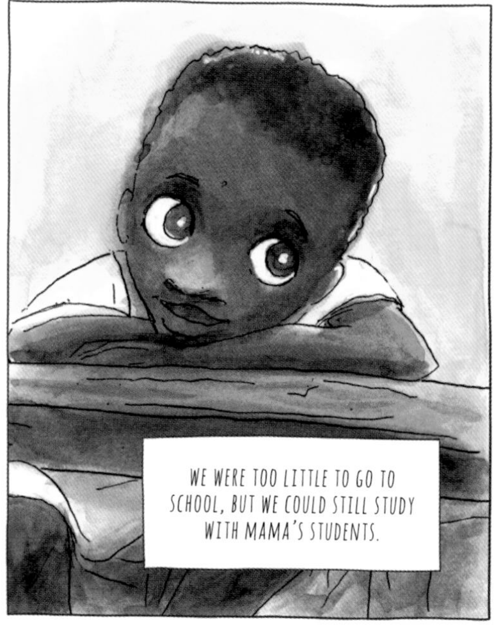
WE WERE TOO LITTLE TO GO TO SCHOOL, BUT WE COULD STILL STUDY WITH MAMA'S STUDENTS.

MY SISTERS AND I MADE SOME FRIENDS.

AT FIRST, WE GOT WATER FROM THE LAKE, AND MY MOTHER HAD TO HEAT IT SO WE COULD DRINK IT.

THEN WE HAD TAP WATER.

ALICE, IT'S STILL A LONG WAIT!

I DON'T KNOW. I THINK WE'RE ALMOST THERE.

I STARTED TO HAVE PROBLEMS WITH MY EYES. THEY HURT.
MORE WAITING! DO WE REALLY HAVE TO?
YES, THE DOCTOR ONLY COMES ONCE A MONTH. WE MUSTN'T MISS HIM.
WE'D GOTTEN UP VERY EARLY TO GET THERE IN TIME.

AND WE WAITED A REALLY LONG TIME.

EVENING CAME AND WE HAD TO LEAVE...
...WITHOUT SEEING THE DOCTOR.

ONE DAY, THEY WOULDN'T LET US GO TO SCHOOL.
MAMA, WHY CAN'T WE GO TO SCHOOL ANYMORE?
REFUGEES AREN'T ALLOWED TO NOW.

YOU DON'T HAVE YOUR TEACHING JOB ANYMORE?

NO, IT'S FINISHED.

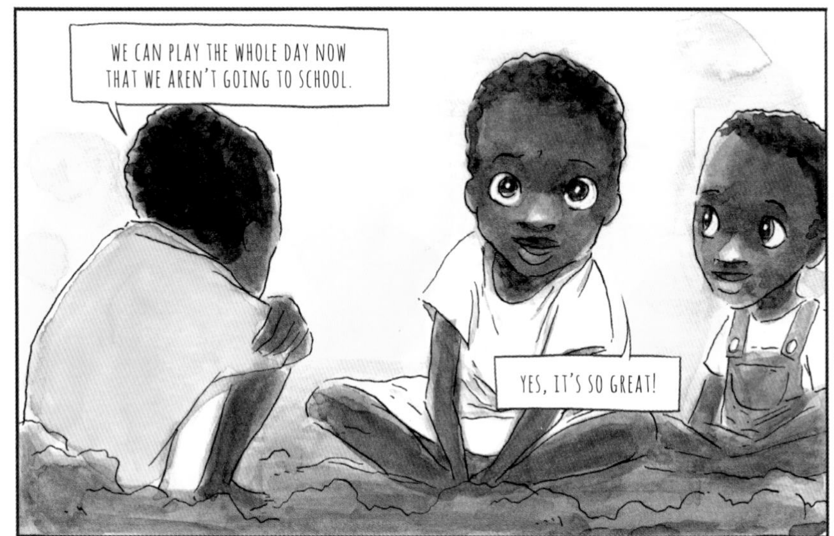
WE CAN PLAY THE WHOLE DAY NOW THAT WE AREN'T GOING TO SCHOOL.
YES, IT'S SO GREAT!

ALICE!

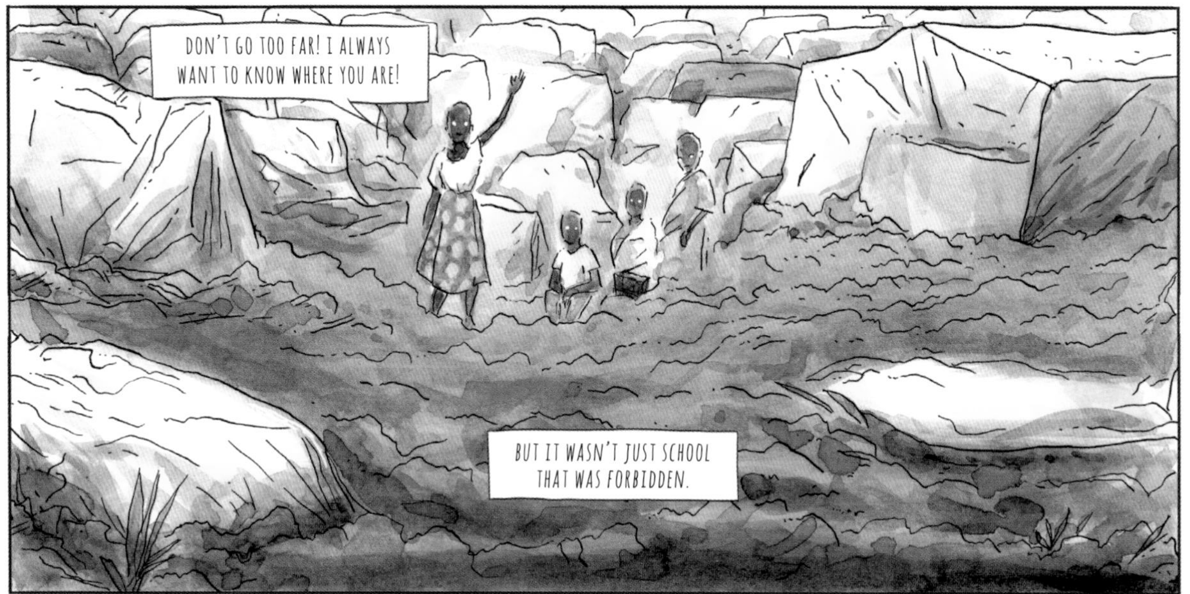
DON'T GO TOO FAR! I ALWAYS WANT TO KNOW WHERE YOU ARE!
BUT IT WASN'T JUST SCHOOL THAT WAS FORBIDDEN.

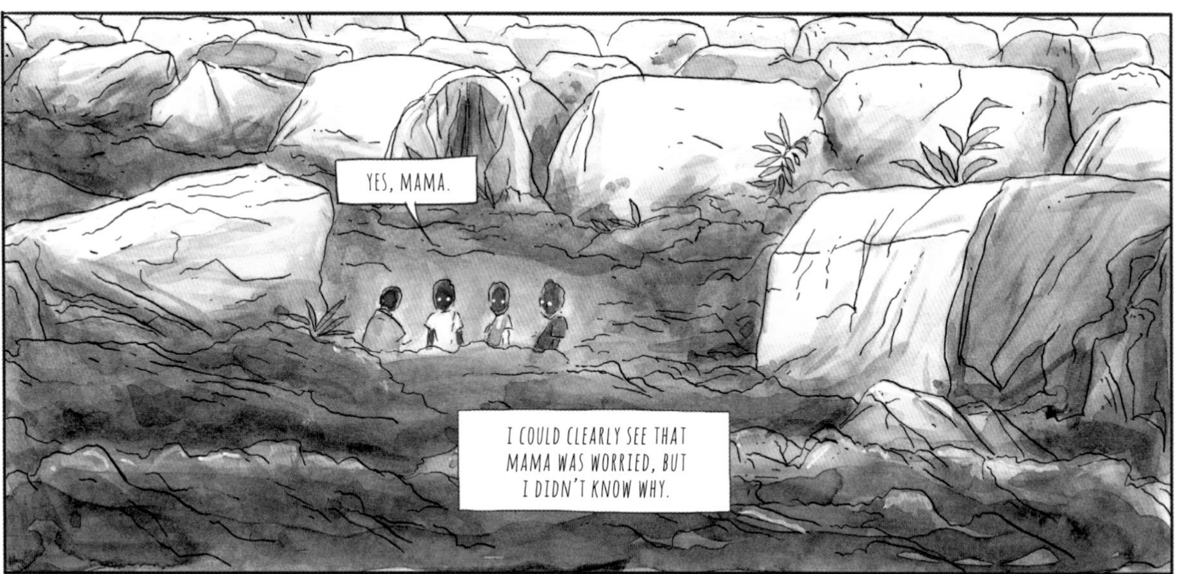
YES, MAMA.
I COULD CLEARLY SEE THAT MAMA WAS WORRIED, BUT I DIDN'T KNOW WHY.

WE LIVED THERE FOR A LITTLE OVER TWO YEARS. THE MOOD IN THE CAMP BECAME STRANGE. WE WATCHED THE GROWNUPS LISTENING TO THE RADIO.

THERE, THAT SHOULD WORK.

A GENERAL SENSE OF ANXIETY SPREAD LITTLE BY LITTLE.

THE SOLDIERS ARE CONTINUING THEIR ADVANCE. IT LOOKS LIKE THEY'RE ABOUT TO ENTER ZAIRE...
FCHH...
FRRR...

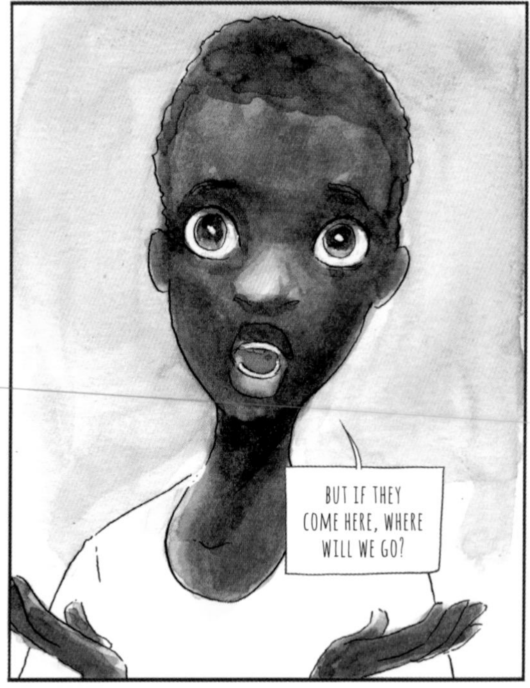

BUT IF THEY COME HERE, WHERE WILL WE GO?

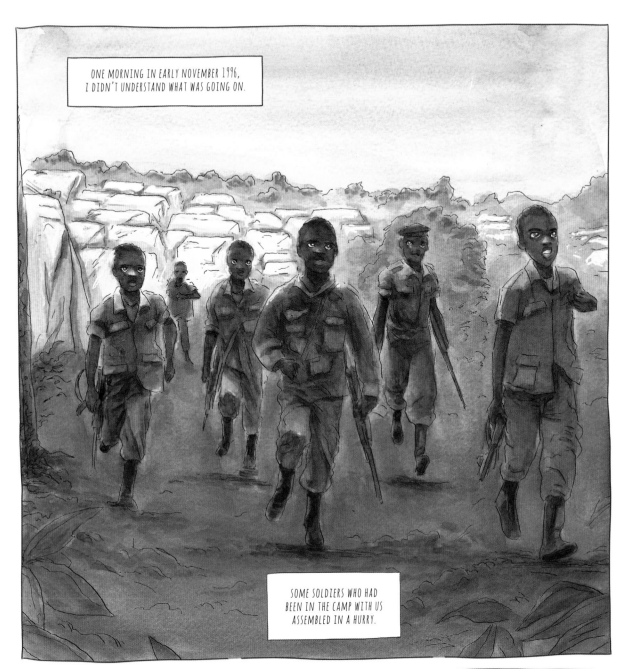

ONE MORNING IN EARLY NOVEMBER 1996,
I DIDN'T UNDERSTAND WHAT WAS GOING ON.

SOME SOLDIERS WHO HAD
BEEN IN THE CAMP WITH US
ASSEMBLED IN A HURRY.

THEY GRABBED THEIR
WEAPONS AND LEFT.

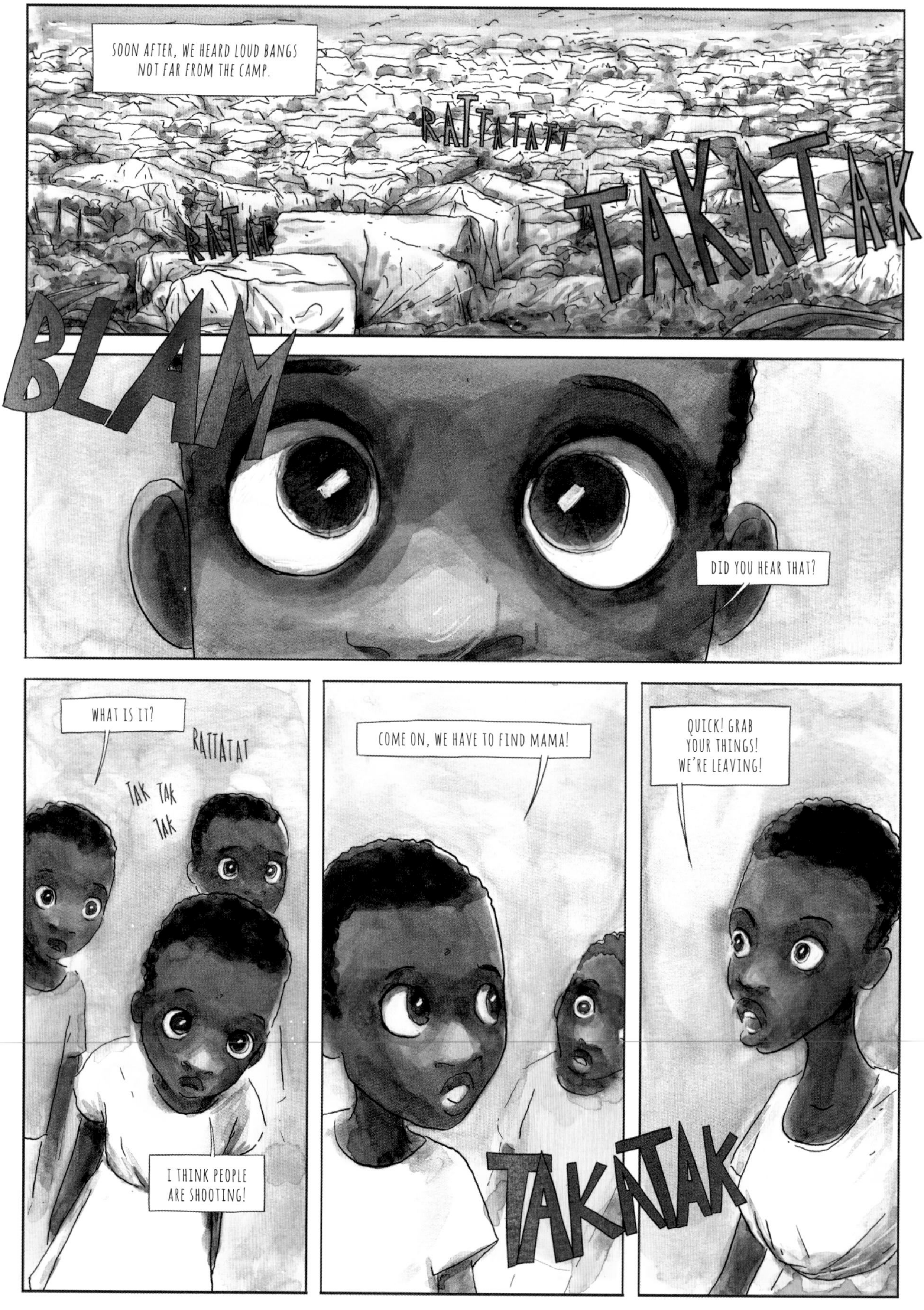

SOON AFTER, WE HEARD LOUD BANGS NOT FAR FROM THE CAMP.

RATTATATT

RATTAT

TAKATAK

BLAM

DID YOU HEAR THAT?

THE SOLDIERS HAD LEFT THE CAMP TO DEAL WITH THE ATTACKERS, GIVING US TIME TO ESCAPE.

TAKATAK
WE WENT INTO THE FOREST.

A VERY DARK FOREST...
I CARRIED THE WATER CONTAINER ON A STRING AROUND MY HEAD.

THERE WAS LOTS OF MUD...

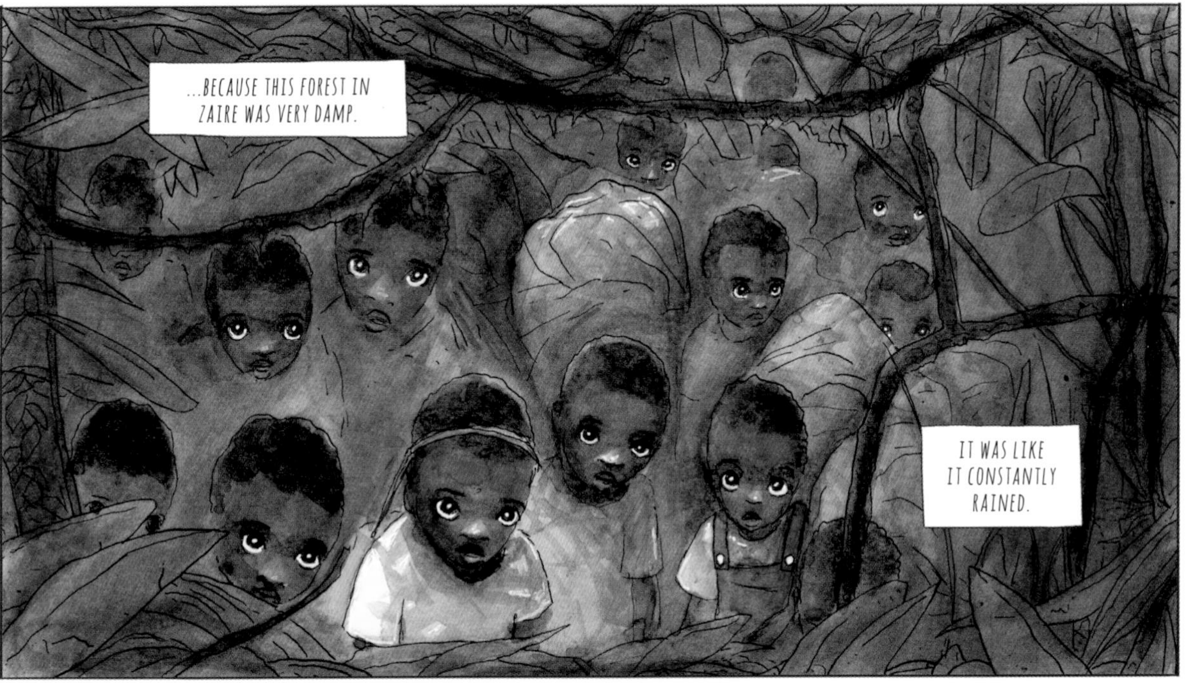
...BECAUSE THIS FOREST IN ZAIRE WAS VERY DAMP.
IT WAS LIKE IT CONSTANTLY RAINED.

WE STOPPED HEARING SHOTS, BUT THE FOREST GOT DARKER AND DARKER. IT WAS TERRIFYING!

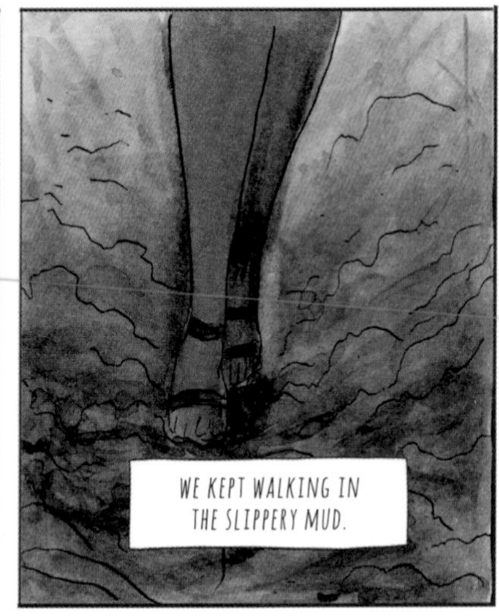
WE KEPT WALKING IN THE SLIPPERY MUD.

WE CAME ACROSS A ROAD
AND LEFT THE FOREST.

AND THEN WE WALKED...

...WALKED...
...WALKED...

...WALKED...
...FOR SO LONG THAT I
LOST ALL SENSE OF TIME.

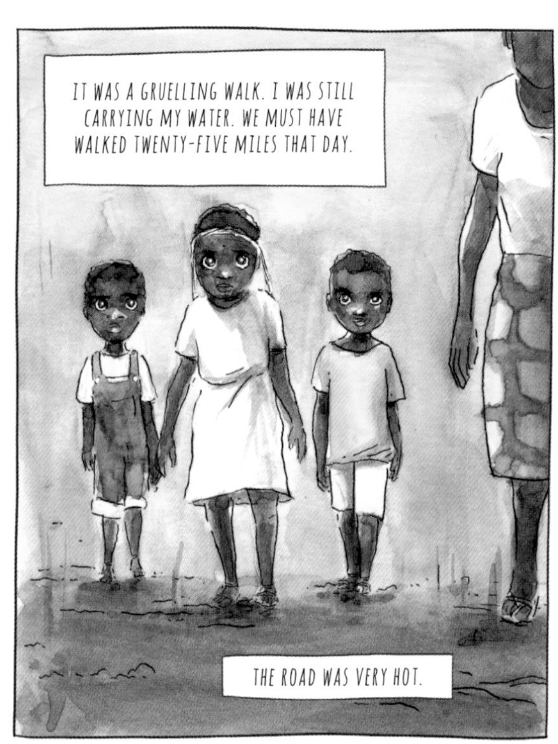
IT WAS A GRUELLING WALK. I WAS STILL CARRYING MY WATER. WE MUST HAVE WALKED TWENTY-FIVE MILES THAT DAY.
THE ROAD WAS VERY HOT.

I'M SO TIRED!
MAMA, MY LEGS HURT!
AND I'M HUNGRY!

I WANT TO STOP AND REST!

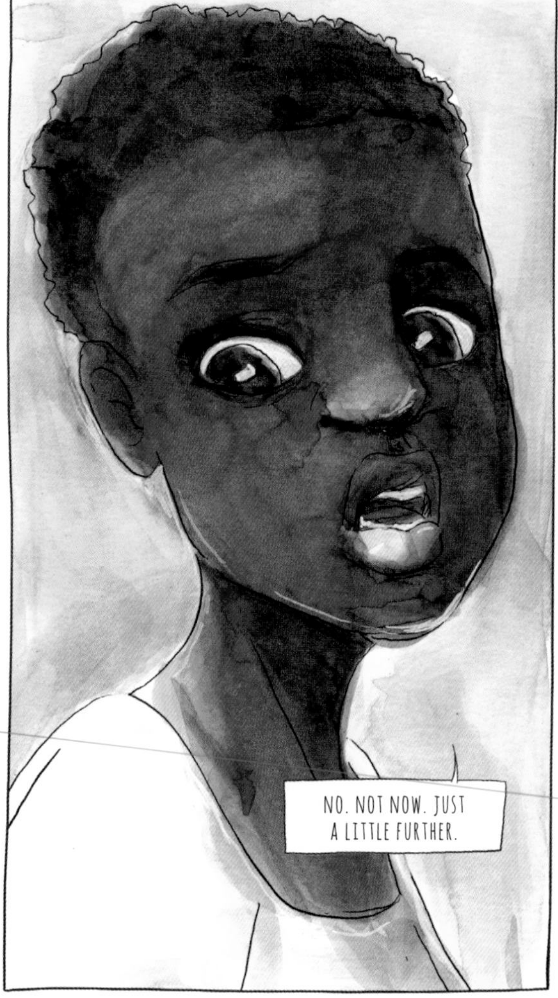
NO. NOT NOW. JUST A LITTLE FURTHER.

HANG IN THERE! WE'LL STOP AT NOON TO EAT, DRINK, AND REST.

WE WERE VERY TIRED, SO SOMETIMES WE GOT REALLY ANNOYING.

MAMA, I WANT US TO STOP!
KEEP THIS UP AND I'LL LEAVE YOU HERE!
MAMA GOT ANGRY, BUT I KNOW IT WAS TO KEEP US GOING.

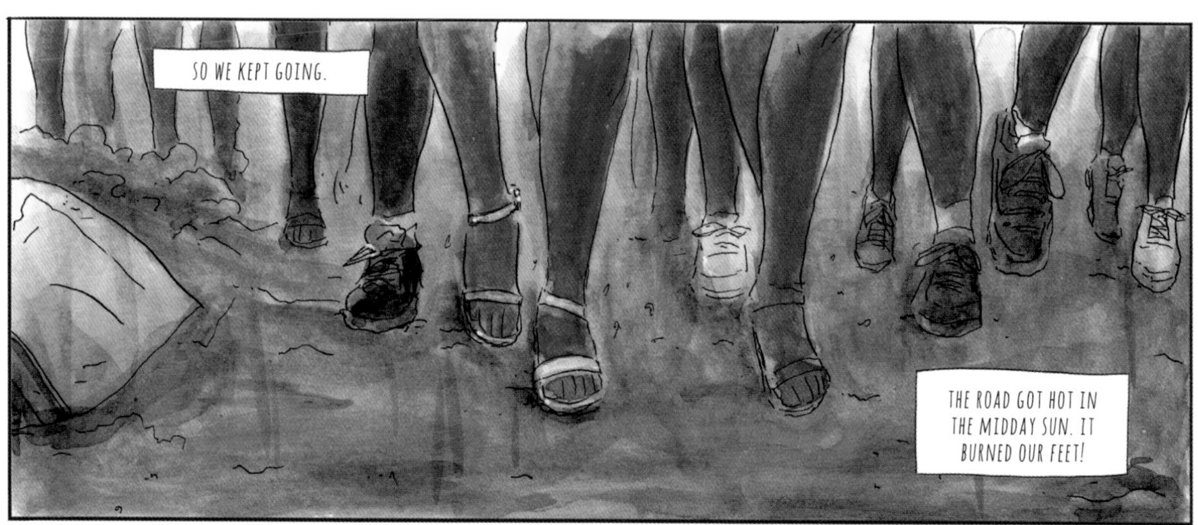
SO WE KEPT GOING.
THE ROAD GOT HOT IN THE MIDDAY SUN. IT BURNED OUR FEET!

WE WERE SO TIRED...

...THAT WE DIDN'T EVEN CRY ANYMORE.

WE DIDN'T TALK ANYMORE...

...WE JUST KEPT WALKING.

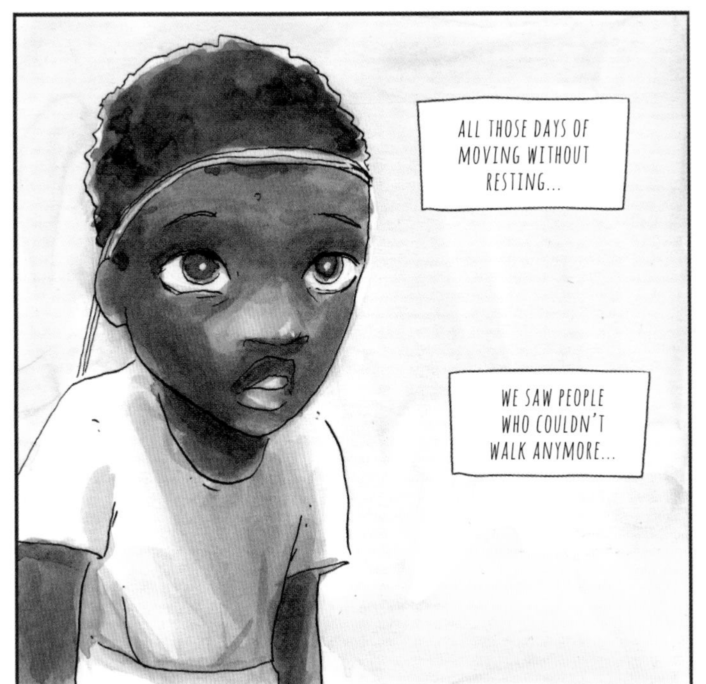
ALL THOSE DAYS OF MOVING WITHOUT RESTING...
WE SAW PEOPLE WHO COULDN'T WALK ANYMORE...

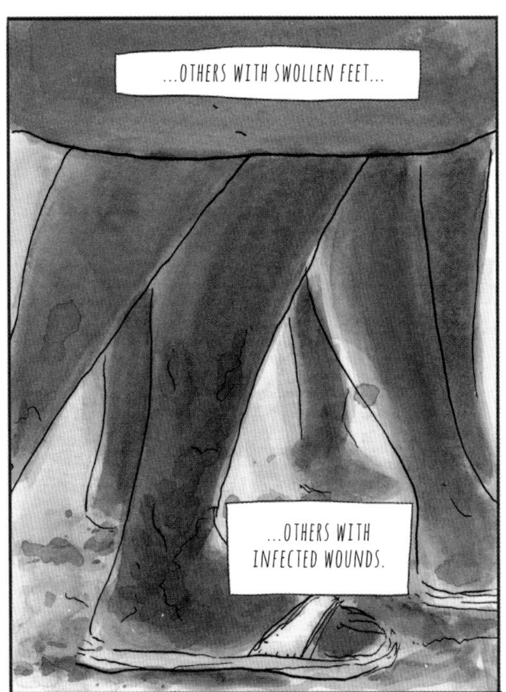
...OTHERS WITH SWOLLEN FEET...
...OTHERS WITH INFECTED WOUNDS.

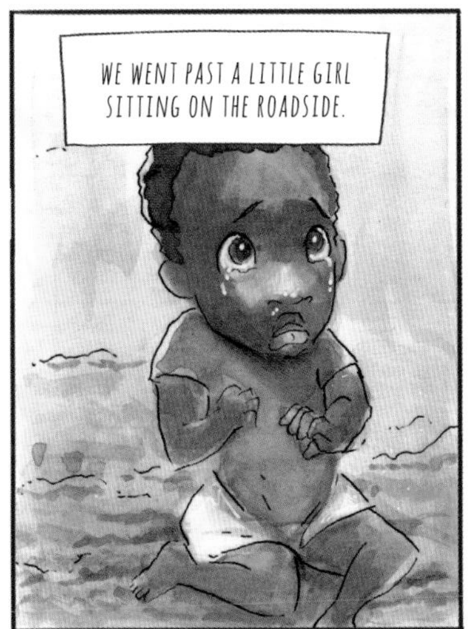
WE WENT PAST A LITTLE GIRL SITTING ON THE ROADSIDE.

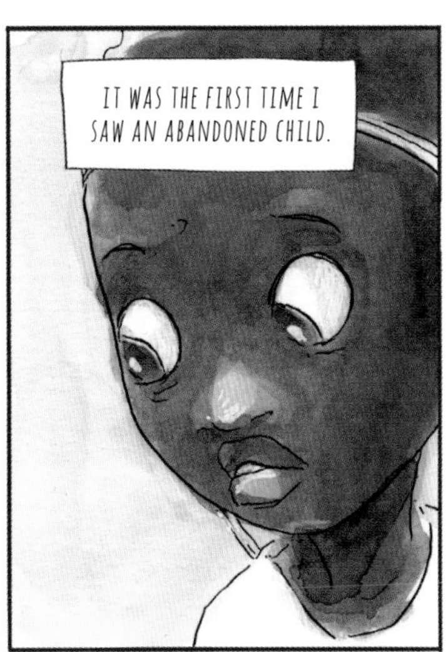
IT WAS THE FIRST TIME I SAW AN ABANDONED CHILD.

I WAS SCARED OF BEING LIKE HER—FINDING MYSELF ALONE.

THERE ARE LOTS OF RIVERS IN ZAIRE.

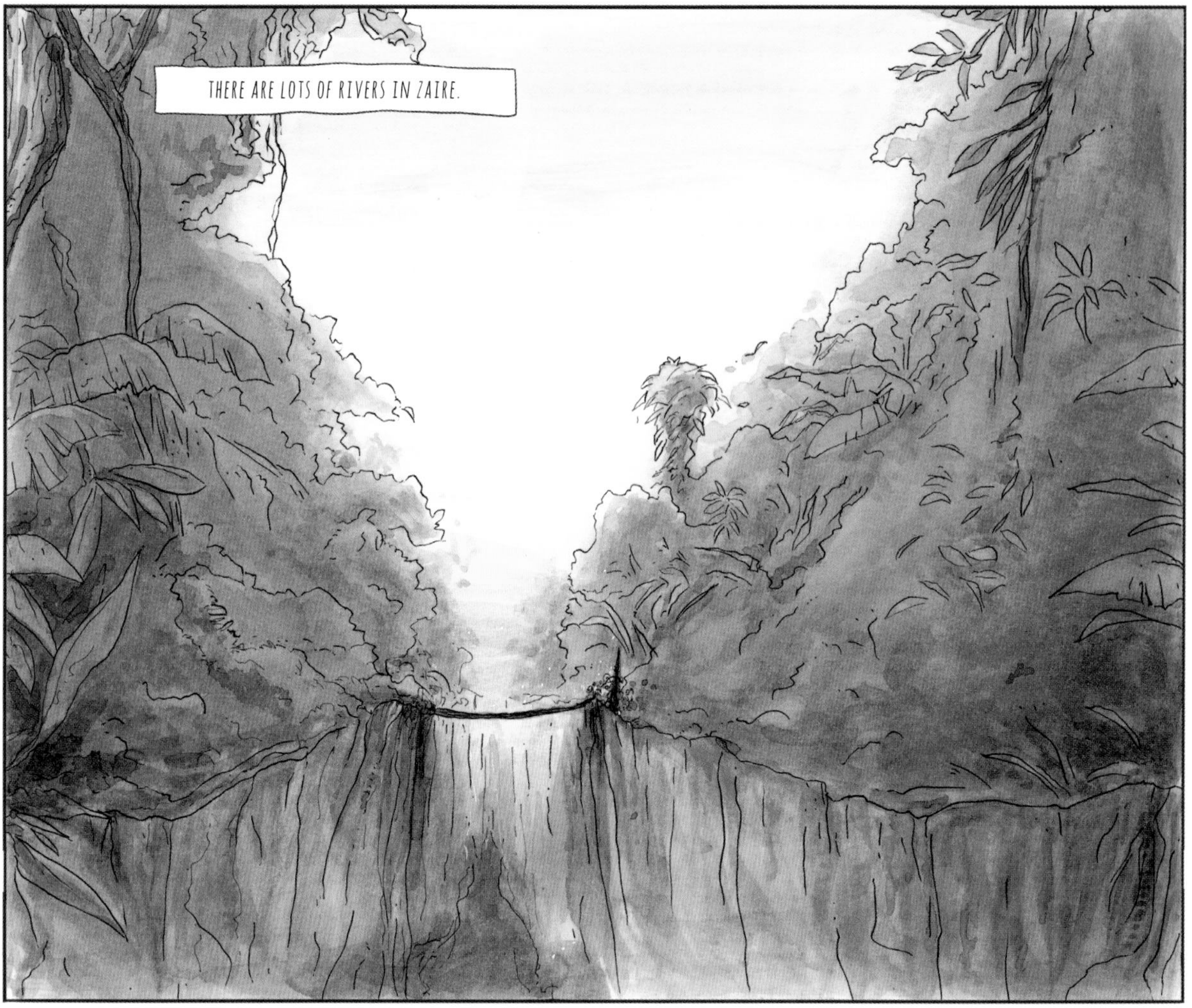

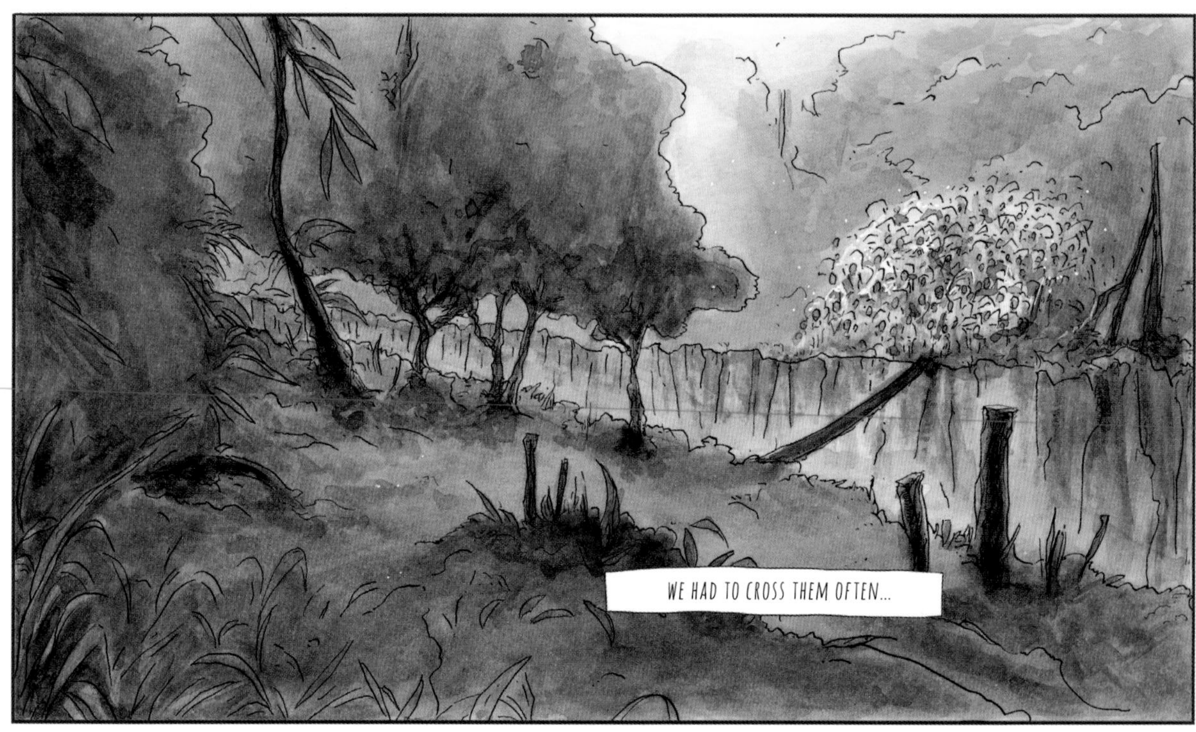
WE HAD TO CROSS THEM OFTEN...

YOU CROSS AFTER THE GENTLEMAN, ALICE.

THE MAN WANTED TO WALK ACROSS.

AAAAAH

ALICE, DON'T THINK ABOUT HIM. LOOK AT ME, EVERYTHING WILL BE OKAY. JUST CROSS SLOWLY ON ALL FOURS.

I WAS TERRIFIED.

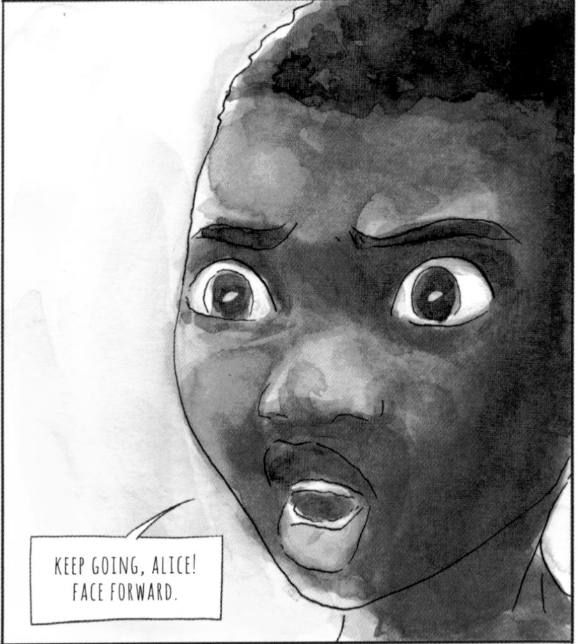
KEEP GOING, ALICE! FACE FORWARD.

I LISTENED TO MY MOTHER'S VOICE...
...BUT I ALSO FELT THE PRESSURE OF THE OTHERS WHO WANTED TO CROSS AFTER ME.

I HAD TO CRAWL...

BUT ALSO GO QUICKLY.

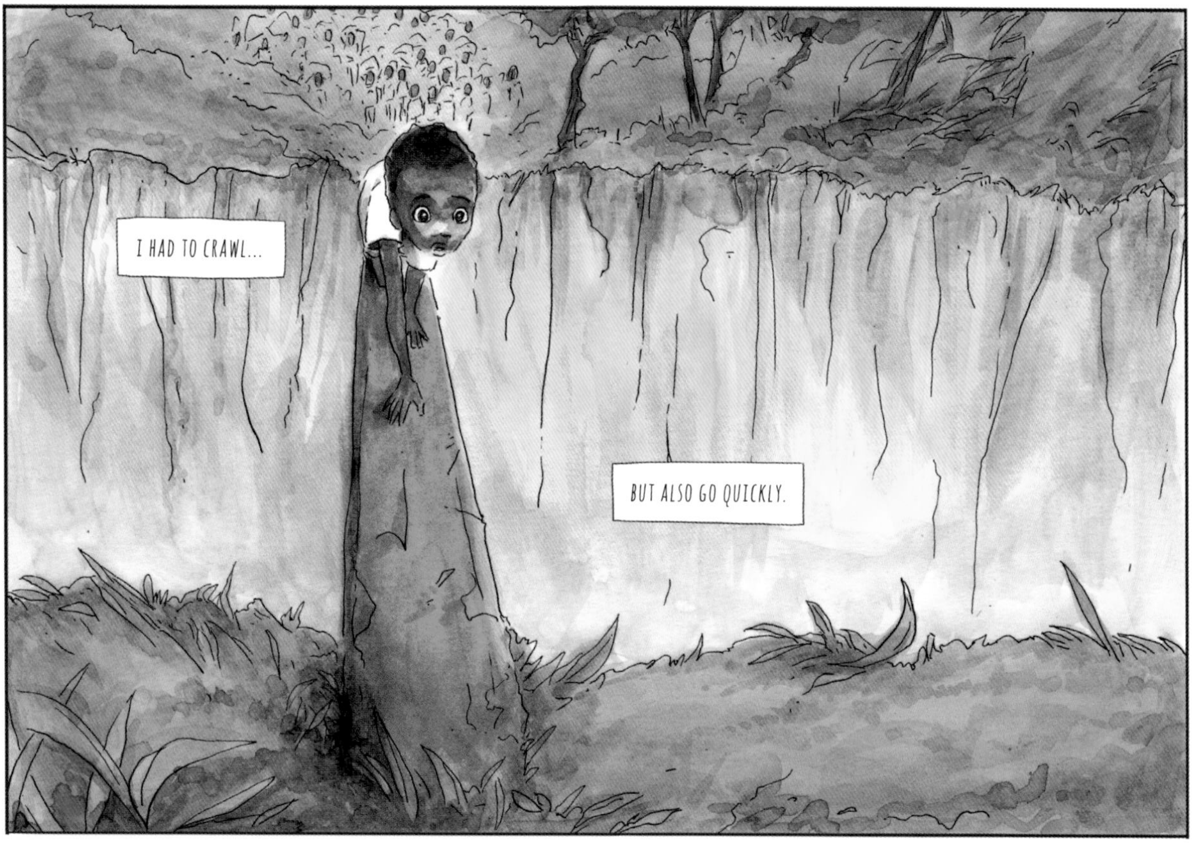

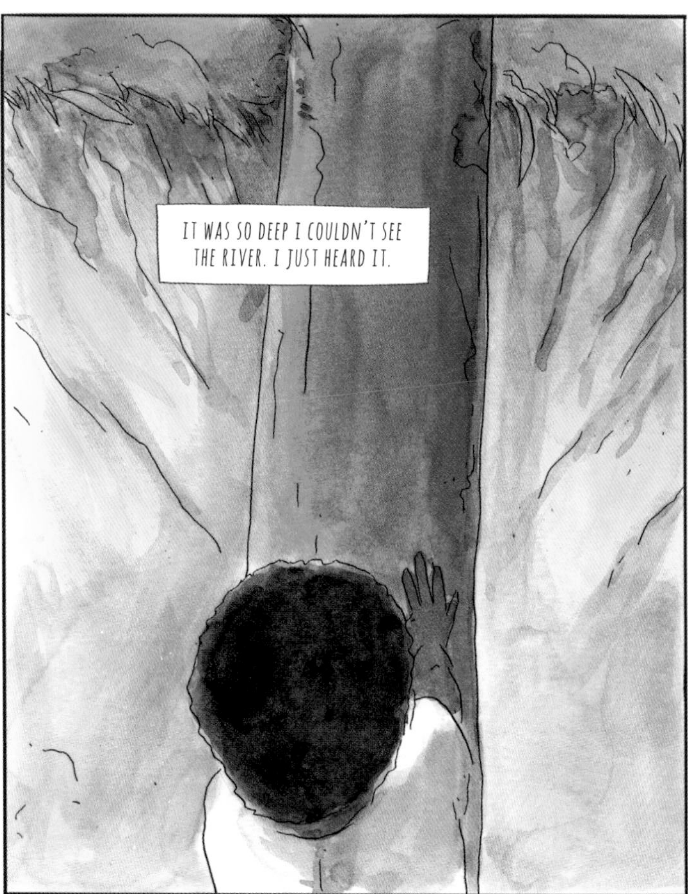

IT WAS SO DEEP I COULDN'T SEE THE RIVER. I JUST HEARD IT.

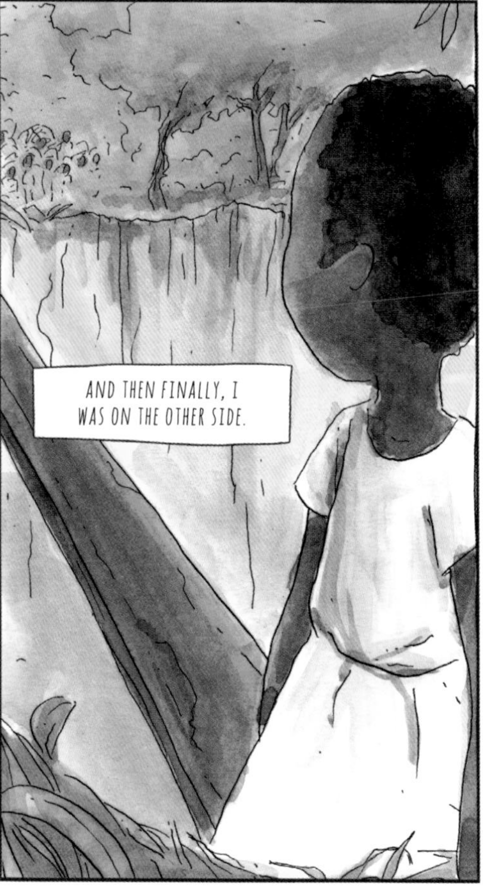

AND THEN FINALLY, I WAS ON THE OTHER SIDE.

January 1997

TINGI-TINGI

MY LITTLE SISTER ALINE WAS SICK, TOO.

SHE WAS ALL YELLOW AND SWOLLEN. SHE HURT EVERYWHERE. MAMA HAD TO CARRY HER.

BUT IN TINGI-TINGI, WE HAD TIME TO RECOVER A LITTLE.

MAMA WORKED FOR THE RED CROSS. SHE HANDED OUT A KIND OF PORRIDGE AND COOKIES.

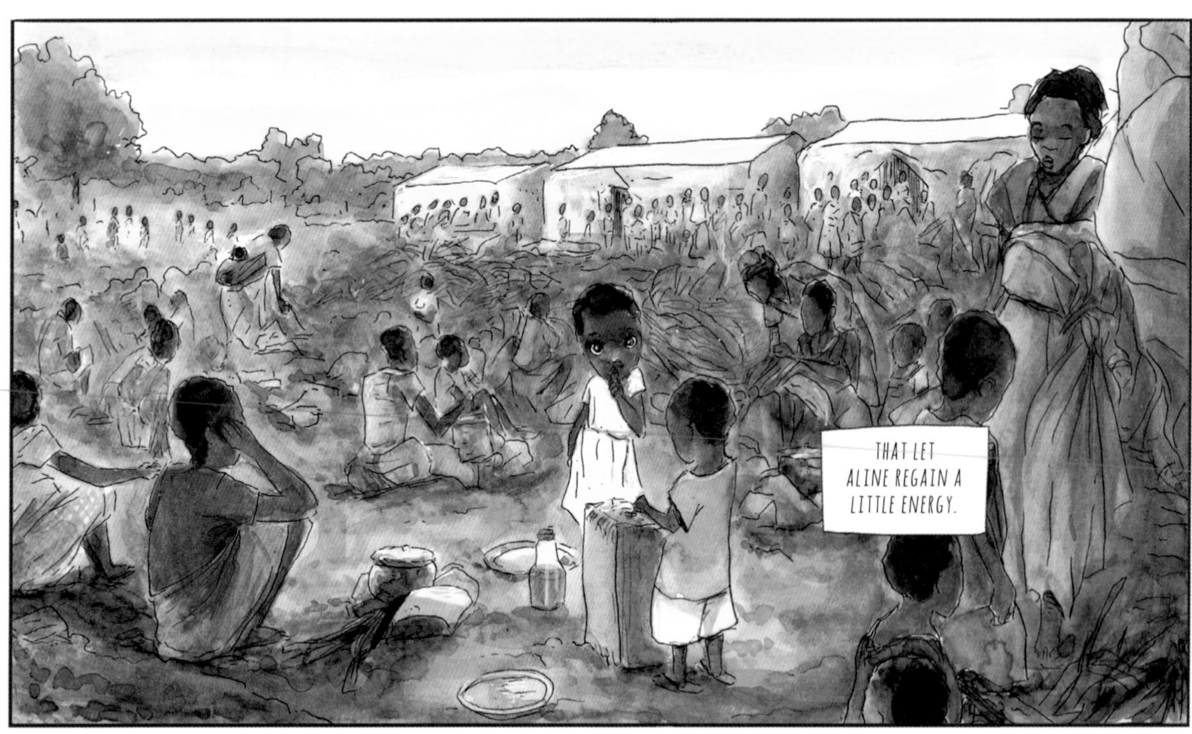
THAT LET ALINE REGAIN A LITTLE ENERGY.

SOMETIMES THE ADULTS HAD TO STEAL FROM THE FIELDS IN ORDER TO EAT.
DON'T MAKE ANY NOISE!

IT'S OKAY. I DON'T SEE ANYONE OUTSIDE!
OKAY, LET'S GO, QUICK!

IT WAS VERY DANGEROUS!

IF THEY WERE CAUGHT, THEY WERE KILLED OR SERIOUSLY WOUNDED AND THE WOMEN WERE RAPED.
CATCH THEM!

WE ALMOST NEVER PLAYED.

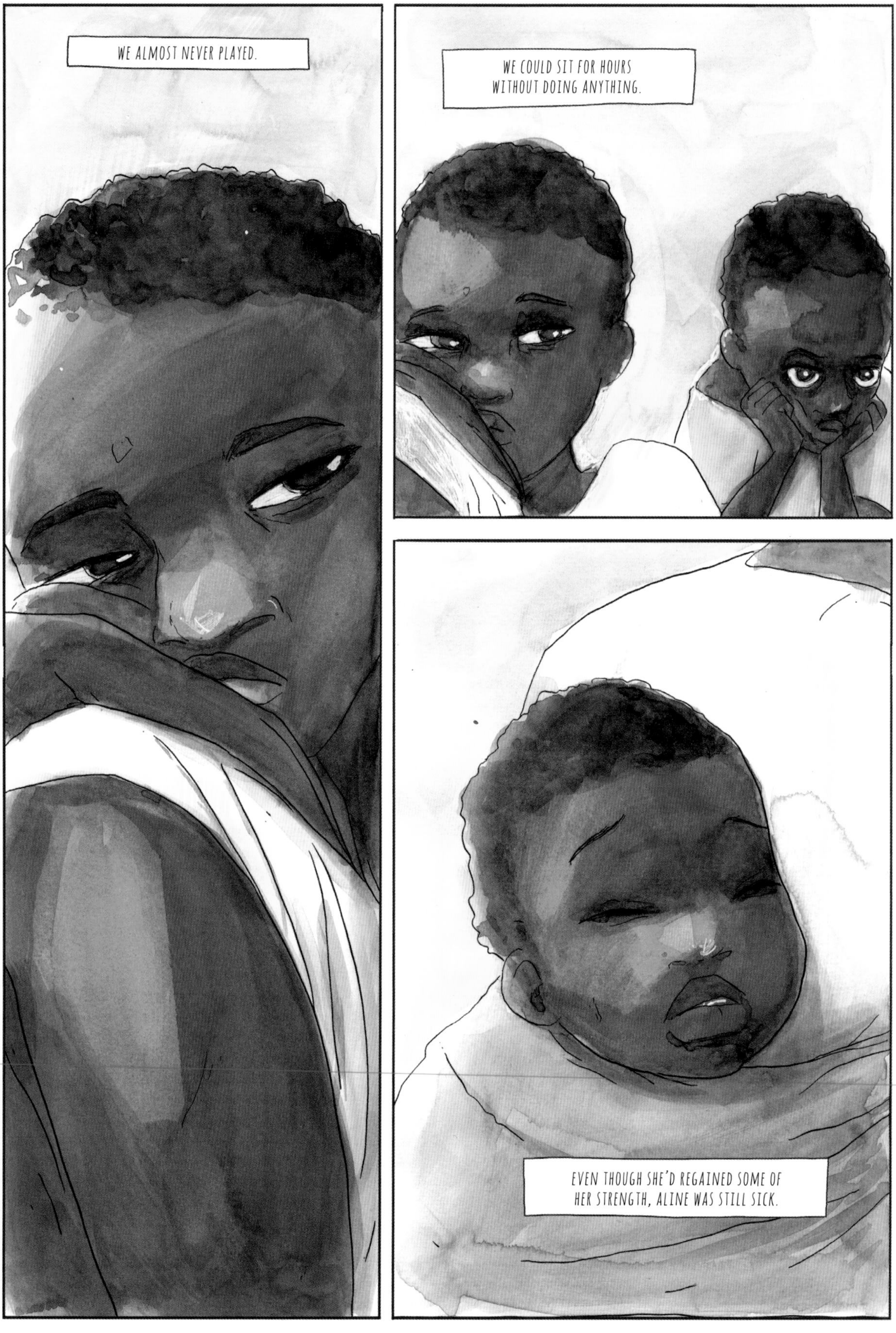

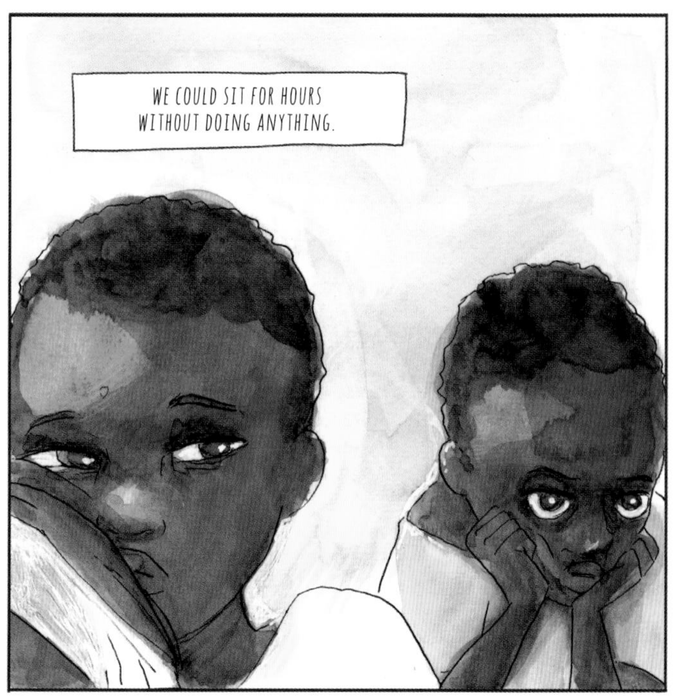

WE COULD SIT FOR HOURS
WITHOUT DOING ANYTHING.

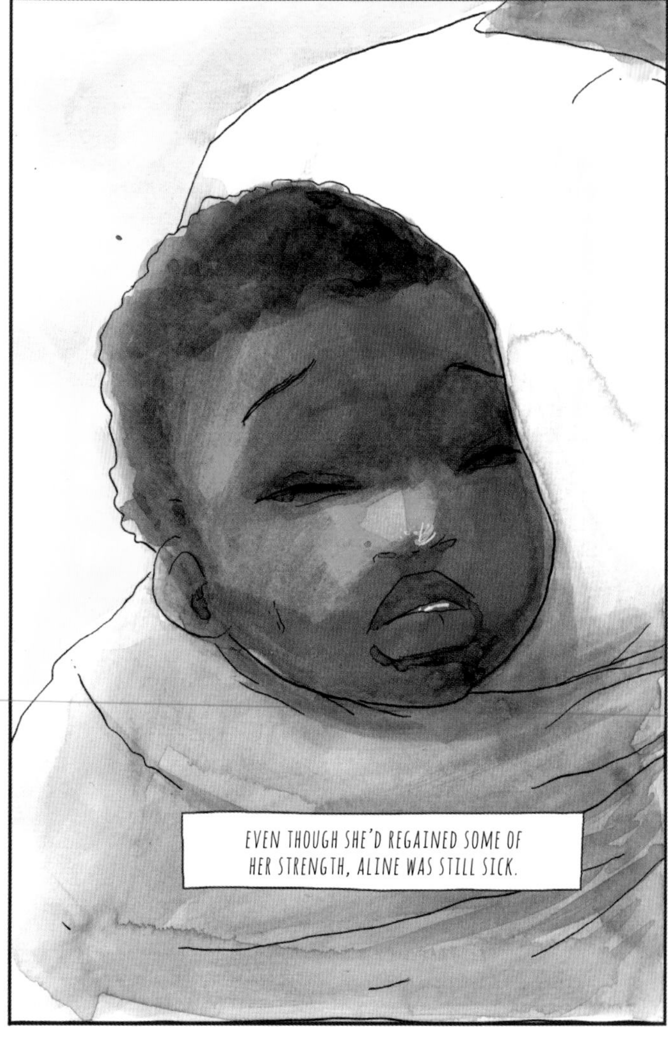

EVEN THOUGH SHE'D REGAINED SOME OF
HER STRENGTH, ALINE WAS STILL SICK.

WE FINALLY BEGAN TO GET USED TO THE TINGI-TINGI CAMP...
...WHEN, IN LATE APRIL 1997...
...DURING A VERY DARK NIGHT...
TAKATAK
BLAM
WE HEARD GUNSHOTS AGAIN!
TAKATAK

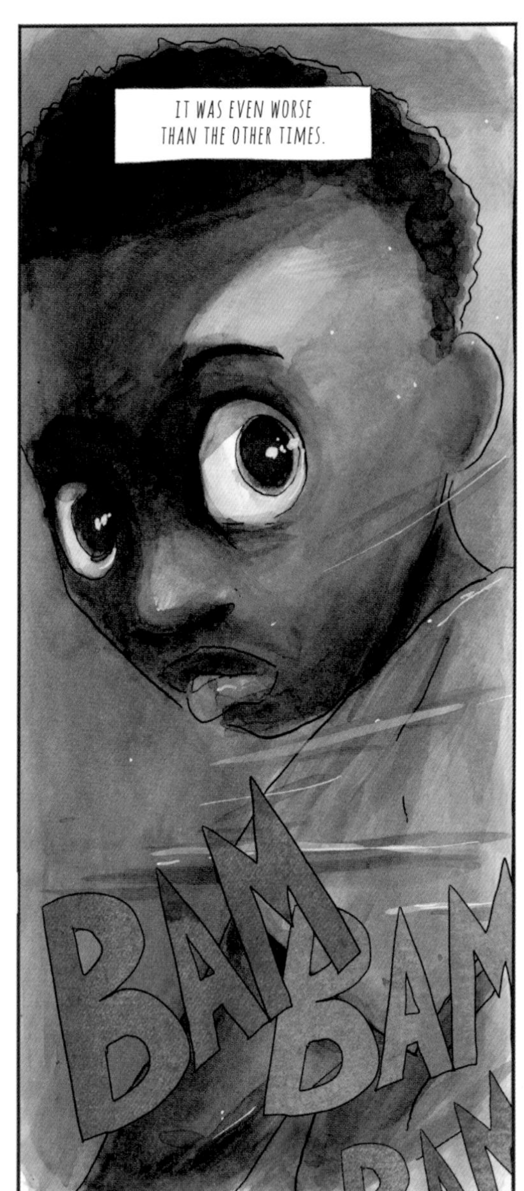
IT WAS EVEN WORSE
THAN THE OTHER TIMES.
BAM
BAM
BAM

PEOPLE RAN IN
ALL DIRECTIONS...
FAMILIES WERE SEPARATED...
RATATAT
RATATAT
MAMA!
THE CRIES OF CHILDREN
CALLING FOR THEIR MOTHERS
WERE THE MOST AWFUL.

PEOPLE WERE GETTING KILLED...
RATATAT

RATATAT

BAM
IT WAS A MASSACRE!
BAM
BAM

PEOPLE WERE BEING TRAMPLED!

RATATATA
RATATA

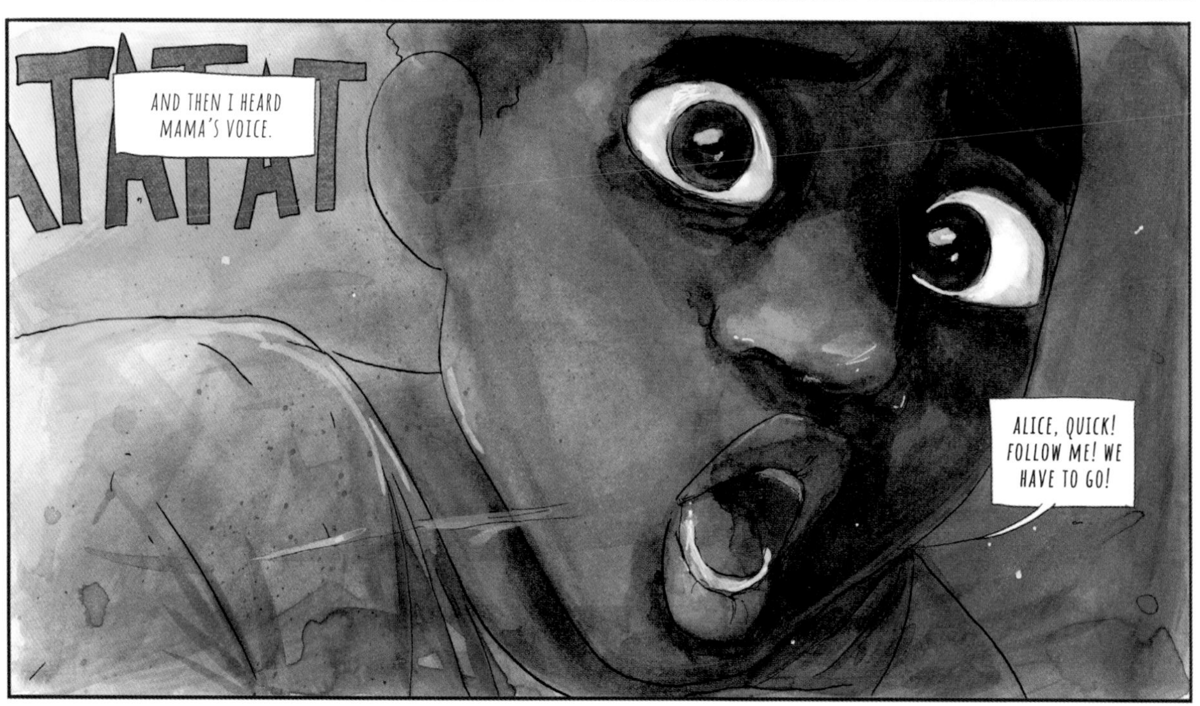
RATATAT
AND THEN I HEARD MAMA'S VOICE.
ALICE, QUICK! FOLLOW ME! WE HAVE TO GO!

RATATAT
BAM
SO I RAN AS QUICKLY AS I COULD!
BAM

BAM
WE FOLLOWED OTHERS WHO WERE RUNNING.
RATATAT
RATATAT

RATATAT
RATATAT
THE SHOTS CONTINUED. IT WAS VERY SCARY!

I DIDN'T REALLY SEE THEM IN THE PANIC, BUT I THINK THE SOLDIERS WHO WERE WITH US COVERED OUR GETAWAY.
THE DAYS THAT FOLLOWED WERE HORRIBLE FOR ME!
WE STARTED WALKING AGAIN.

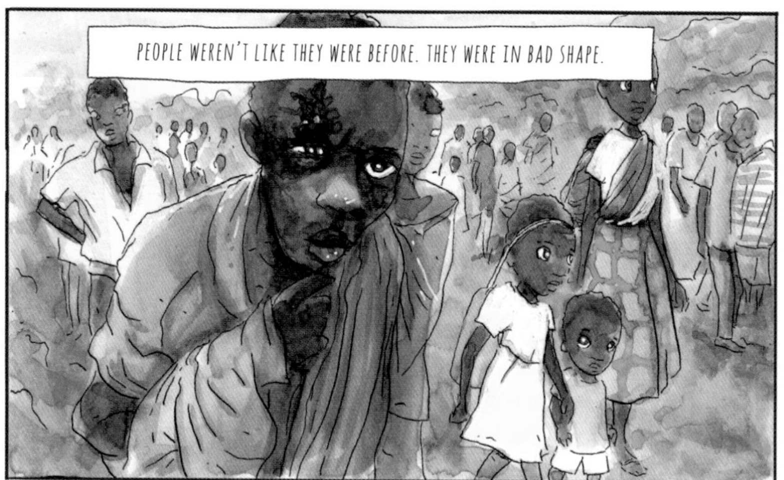
PEOPLE WEREN'T LIKE THEY WERE BEFORE. THEY WERE IN BAD SHAPE.

MANY CHILDREN WERE ALONE.
SOMETIMES THERE WERE TWO. THEN THE BIGGER ONE CARED FOR THE LITTLER ONE.

WE WERE LUCKY ENOUGH TO STILL BE TOGETHER— MY LITTLE SISTERS, MY MAMA, AND ME.
WE CONTINUED THE LONG JOURNEY.

...I SLEPT...

...THAT WAS ALL...

ACTUALLY, NO, I DIDN'T SLEEP AT NIGHT ANYMORE.

ALTHOUGH I TRIED...

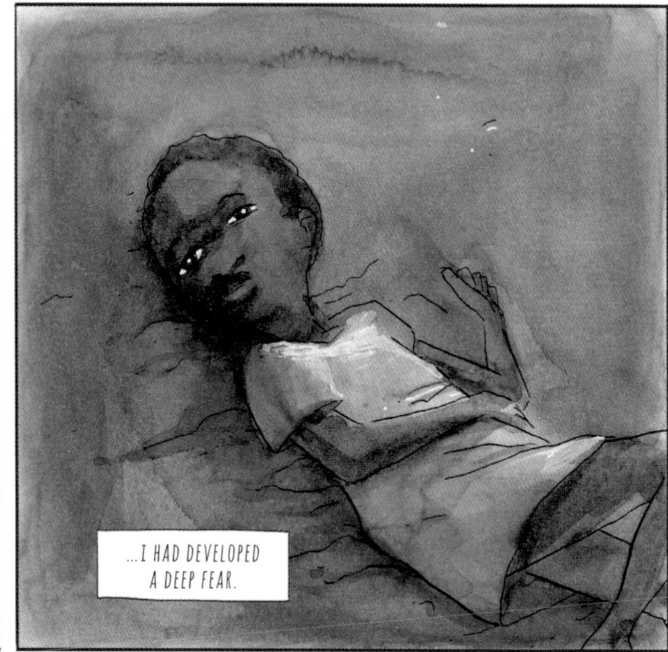
...I HAD DEVELOPED A DEEP FEAR.

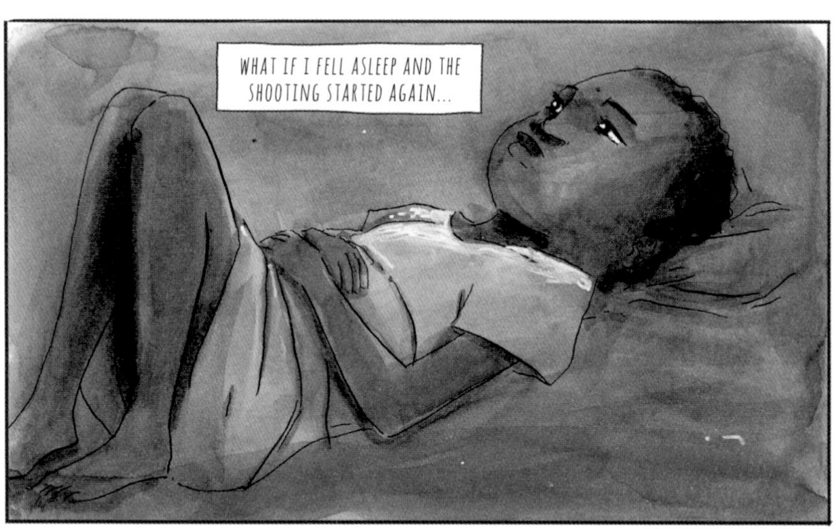
WHAT IF I FELL ASLEEP AND THE SHOOTING STARTED AGAIN...

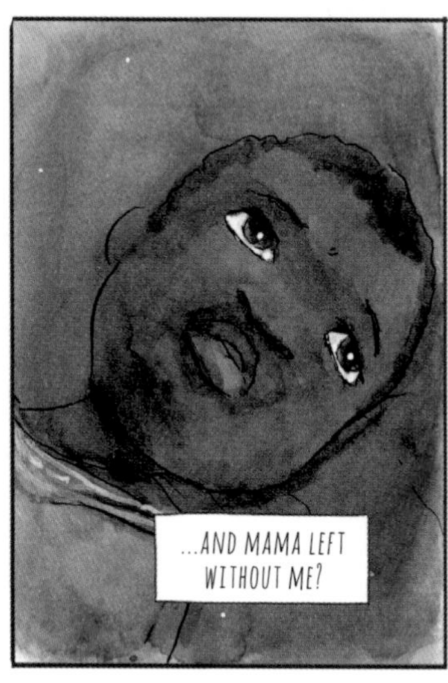
...AND MAMA LEFT WITHOUT ME?

WE KEPT WALKING
DURING THE DAY...

...WE RESTED ONLY
AT NIGHT...

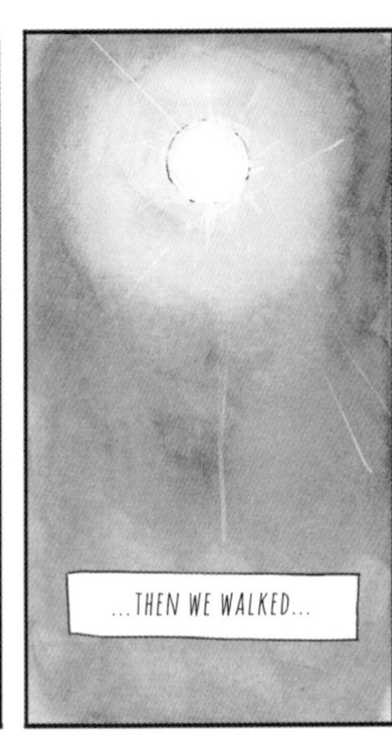
...THEN WE WALKED...

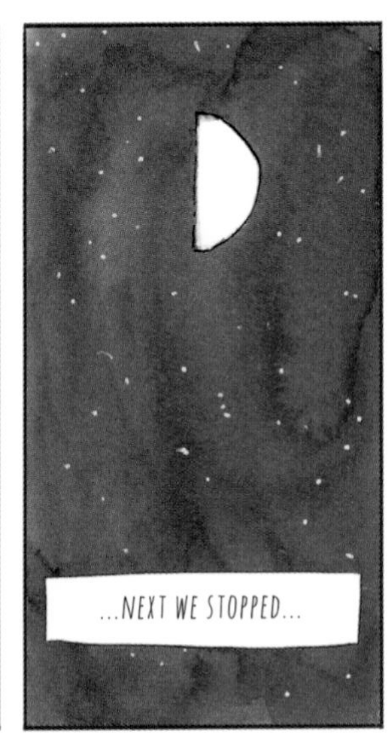
...NEXT WE STOPPED...

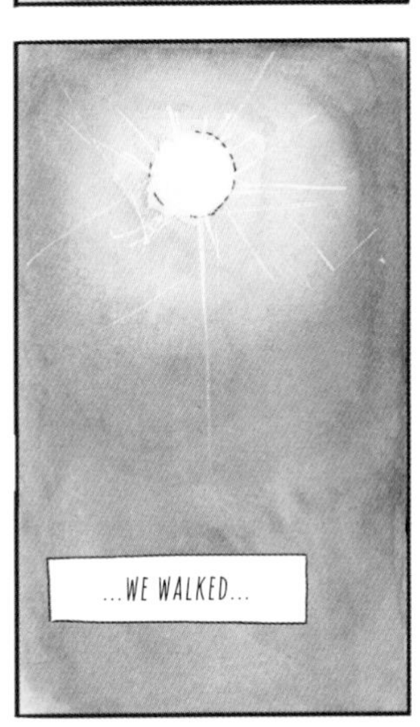
...WE WALKED...

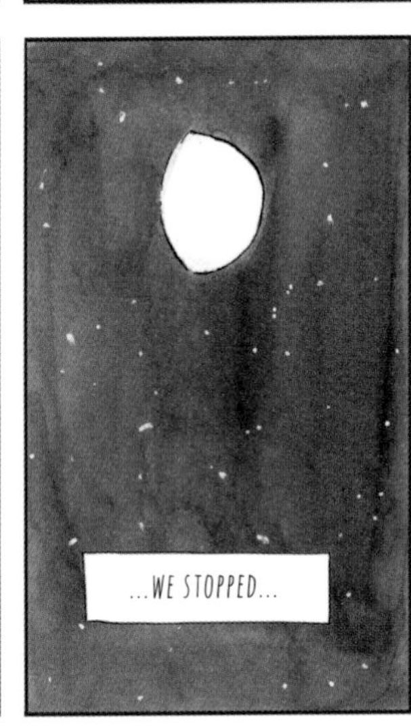
...WE STOPPED...

...WE MOVED ON...

...WE SLEPT. EXCEPT
WHEN THE MOON
WAS FULL...

THEN, I WAS EVEN MORE SCARED...
...BECAUSE THEN I
COULD SEE EVERYTHING
AROUND ME.

August 1997

MBANDAKA

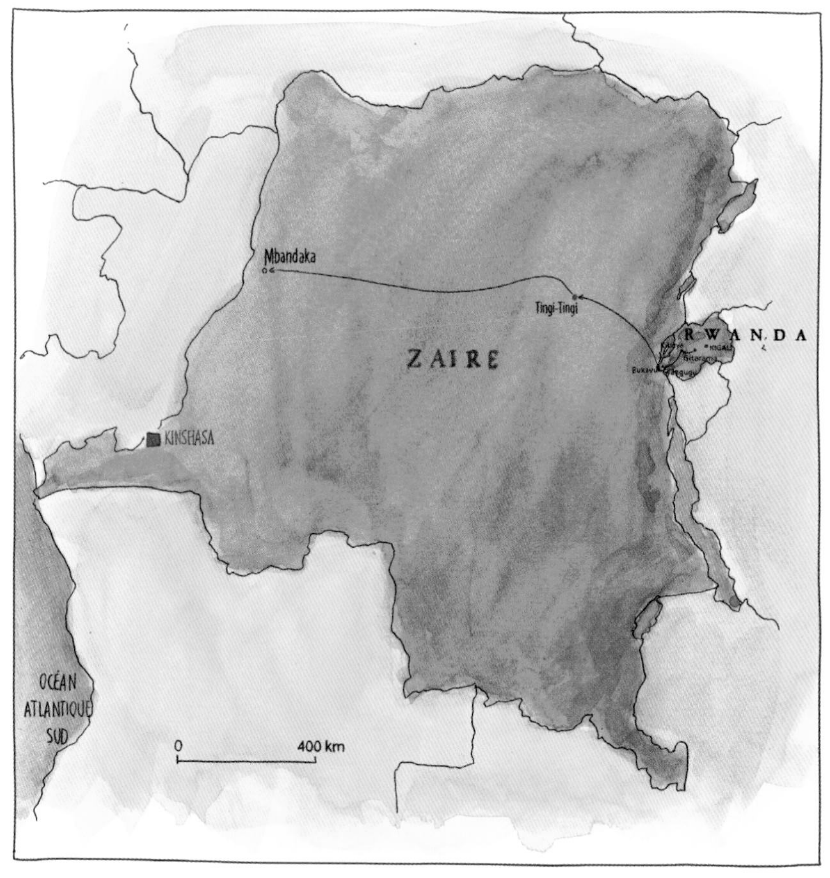

AFTER ABOUT THREE MONTHS OF WALKING, WE GOT TO MBANDAKA.

I'D STARTED TO GET BUMPS ON MY FINGERS.

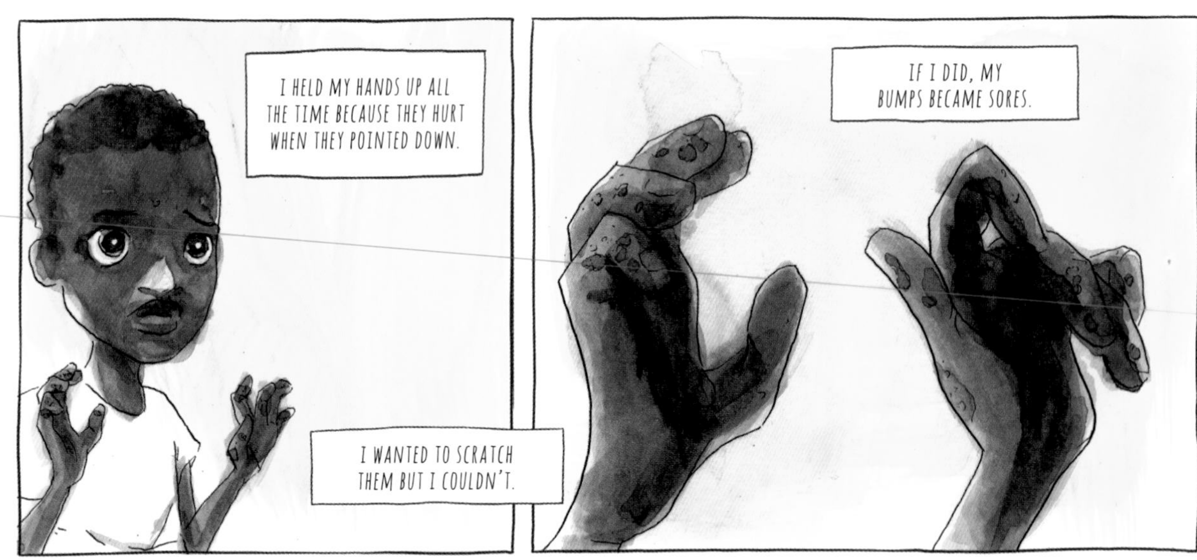

I HELD MY HANDS UP ALL THE TIME BECAUSE THEY HURT WHEN THEY POINTED DOWN.
I WANTED TO SCRATCH THEM BUT I COULDN'T.
IF I DID, MY BUMPS BECAME SORES.

THERE WERE DOCTORS FROM THE RED CROSS THERE.
PEOPLE LINED UP TO SEE THEM.

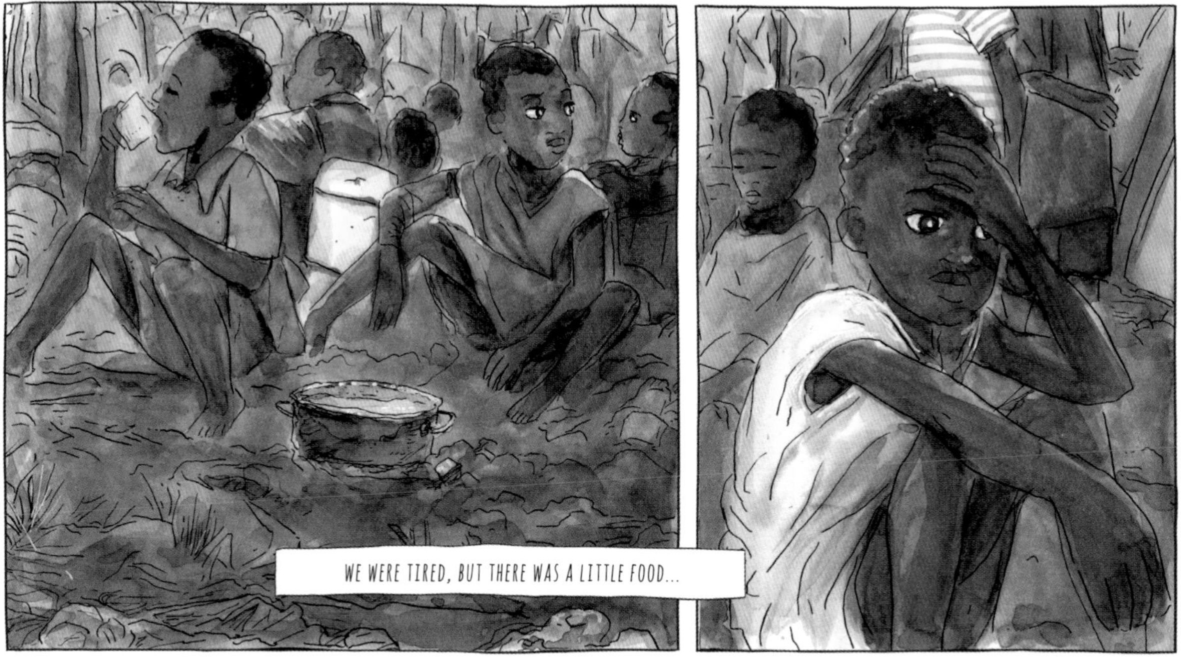
WE WERE TIRED, BUT THERE WAS A LITTLE FOOD...

...PLUS FISH THAT PEOPLE CAUGHT IN THE RIVER.

WE HAD TO WAIT A LONG TIME TO SEE THE DOCTOR.

ANOTHER DAY SPENT
WAITING IN LINE.

NIGHT'S COMING.
WE SHOULD GO HOME.
OKAY. ANOTHER DAY
WITHOUT SEEING THE DOCTOR.

WE'LL TRY ANOTHER DAY.

IT WAS AROUND TWO WEEKS AFTER WE'D GOTTEN TO MBANDAKA. IT MUST HAVE BEEN ABOUT 9 A.M.
THE LINE FOR SEEING THE DOCTOR WAS ALREADY LONG.

BACK IN LINE.
AS USUAL.

WHEN SUDDENLY...

CLIC

TAKATAKATAK
TAK
TAK

TAKATAKATAK
BAM
TAKATAK
IT WAS THE MOST HORRIFYING MORNING OF MY LIFE.

IT WAS A NEW ATTACK, THE MOST VIOLENT OF THEM ALL.
TAKATAK
RATATA
BAM
QUICK! FOLLOW ME! WE HAVE TO FIND MAMA!

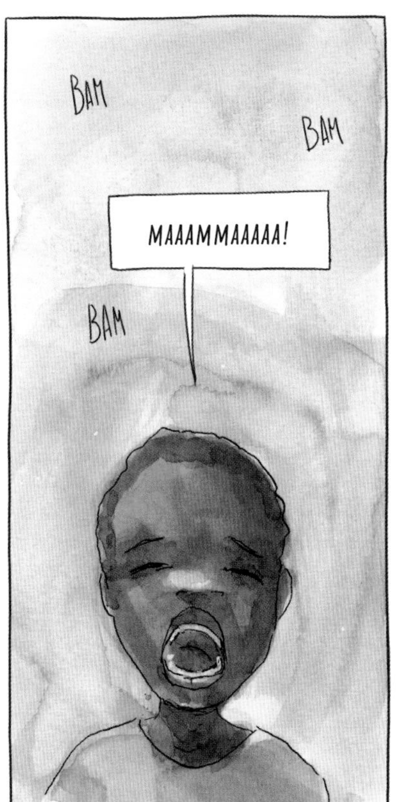

BUT MAMA WASN'T THERE.
THERE WAS ALMOST NO ONE LEFT...

TAKATAKATA

BLAM

...ALMOST NO ONE LEFT ALIVE.

LET'S KEEP LOOKING.

I THINK I SAW SOME PEOPLE THIS WAY...

...

WHO ARE ALL THESE PEOPLE?
I DON'T KNOW. PEOPLE FROM THE CAMP?

MAMA ISN'T HERE.

BUT WHY'RE THEY ALL SLEEPING?

THEY'RE NOT SLEEPING...

THEY'RE STILL SHOOTING! WE'RE GOING TO DIE!
LET'S GET OUT OF HERE!

IT LOOKS LIKE EVERYONE
WENT INTO THE FOREST.

OH! LOOK!

THAT LOOKS LIKE MAMA'S SANDAL!

LET'S GO!

WE STILL HEARD SHOTS BEING FIRED, EVEN IN THE FOREST.

TAKATAKATAK

BAM BAM BAM

WE STILL HAVEN'T SEEN MAMA. WE HAVEN'T ACTUALLY SEEN ANYONE.

NO, NOT YET...

LISTEN! IT SOUNDS LIKE THERE'S WATER UP AHEAD.

ALICE!

DID MAMA ABANDON US?

I'LL PULL YOU OUT OF THERE!
SHE DID. SHE ABANDONED US!

I TRIED NOT TO CRY.
COME ON!

I KNEW THERE WAS NO WAY MAMA WOULD HAVE ABANDONED US!
I CAN'T DO IT!

MAMA LEFT WITHOUT U-- ARGH!
ALL I WANTED WAS TO FIND HER AND HAVE HER HELP ME GET MY LITTLE SISTER OUT OF THERE.

THEN I RECOGNIZED A MAN
MY PARENTS KNEW WELL.
I WAS SO HAPPY I
STARTED TO CRY.

MY SISTER'S GOING TO DROWN
IN THE MUD! PLEASE HELP ME!

IF YOU'RE AFRAID SHE'LL DROWN
BEFORE YOU, HERE YOU GO... I'LL HELP...

AAAAAH

THIS WAY, YOU'LL DIE TOGETHER.

WHY WOULD I HELP SOMEONE ELSE'S CHILDREN WHEN I'VE LOST MY OWN?!

THERE I WAS, UP TO MY NECK IN MUD, TOO.

COUGH! COUGH!
HANG ON, ADELINE! WE'RE GOING TO GET OUT.
WE AREN'T FAR FROM THE SHORE.
I'M GOING TO TRY TO GRAB ONTO SOMETHING.

THERE! IT'S SOME KIND OF ROOT!

GOT IT!

I'M SINKING!
HANG ON! I'LL GET YOU.

ARGH!

ADELINE!

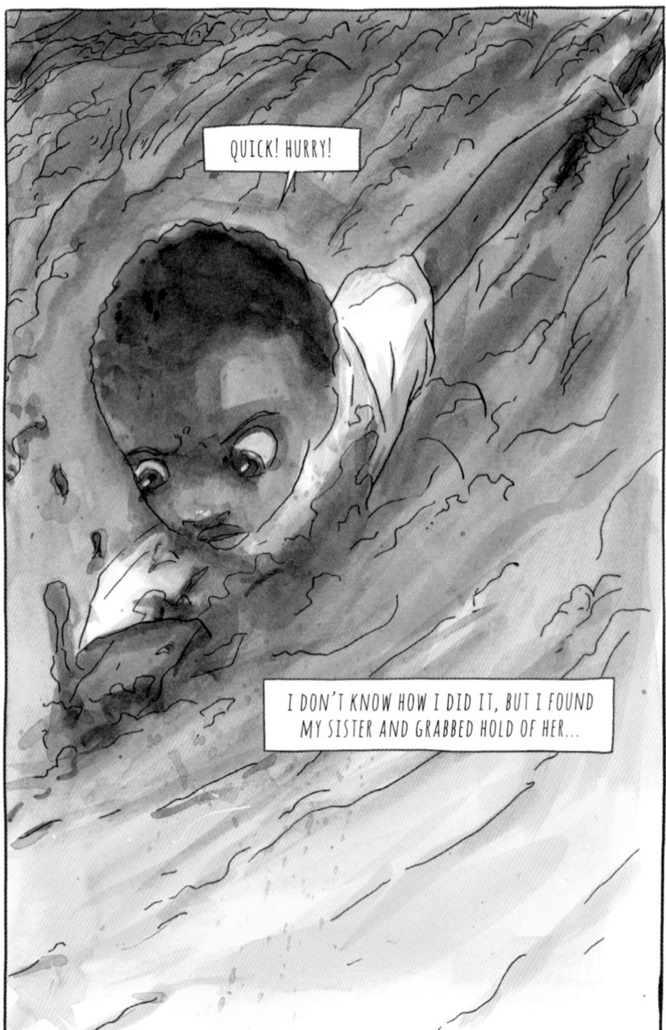
QUICK! HURRY!
I DON'T KNOW HOW I DID IT, BUT I FOUND MY SISTER AND GRABBED HOLD OF HER...

...THEN I MANAGED TO GET HER OUT OF THE MUD. BUT I DIDN'T KNOW IF SHE'D BEEN UNDER FOR TOO LONG.

ADELINE, CAN YOU HEAR ME?
IF SHE'D STAYED THERE ANY LONGER...
...I THINK SHE WOULD'VE DROWNED, BECAUSE SHE COUGHED UP A LOT OF MUD.
YOU OKAY, ADELINE?
YES, BUT I FEEL FULL.
SHE'D EVEN SWALLOWED SOME OF IT.

WE WEREN'T IN THE MUD FOR VERY LONG,
BUT IT SEEMED LIKE FOREVER TO ME.

WE KEPT LOOKING FOR MAMA AS WE
WALKED DEEPER INTO THE JUNGLE.

WE DIDN'T CALL OUT FOR HER ANYMORE BECAUSE WE WERE AFRAID ANOTHER BAD PERSON WOULD FIND US.
IN FACT, WE BARELY TALKED AT ALL.

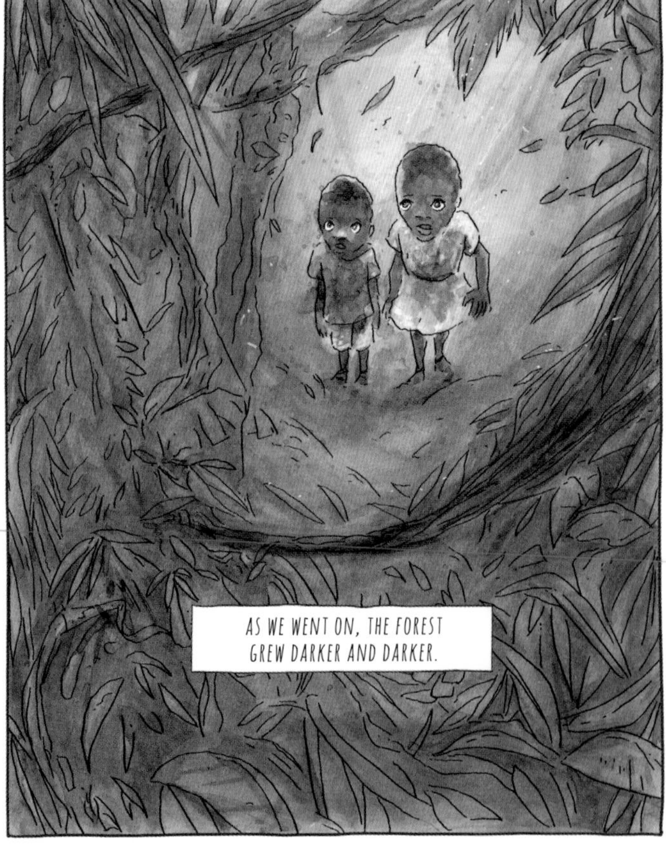

AS WE WENT ON, THE FOREST GREW DARKER AND DARKER.

WE WALKED THE WHOLE DAY IN SILENCE.

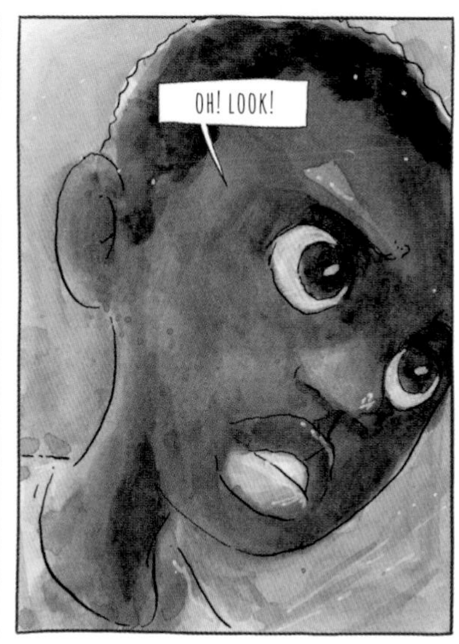
OH! LOOK!

THERE'S SOMETHING OVER THERE!
LOOKS LIKE A BAG AND AN OLD POT.

IT'S SOME SORT OF FLOUR.

YES, IT'S SORGHUM FLOUR.
SO, WE CAN EAT IT?

I CAN'T REMEMBER HOW I DID IT, BUT I MANAGED TO LIGHT A FIRE.
WE ATE A MUSH MADE FROM THE FLOUR AND WATER.

AFTER LOOKING FOR OUR MAMA THE WHOLE DAY, WE TRIED TO SLEEP. BUT SLEEP WOULDN'T COME.
THAT WAS THE FIRST NIGHT WE SPENT ALONE IN THE JUNGLE.

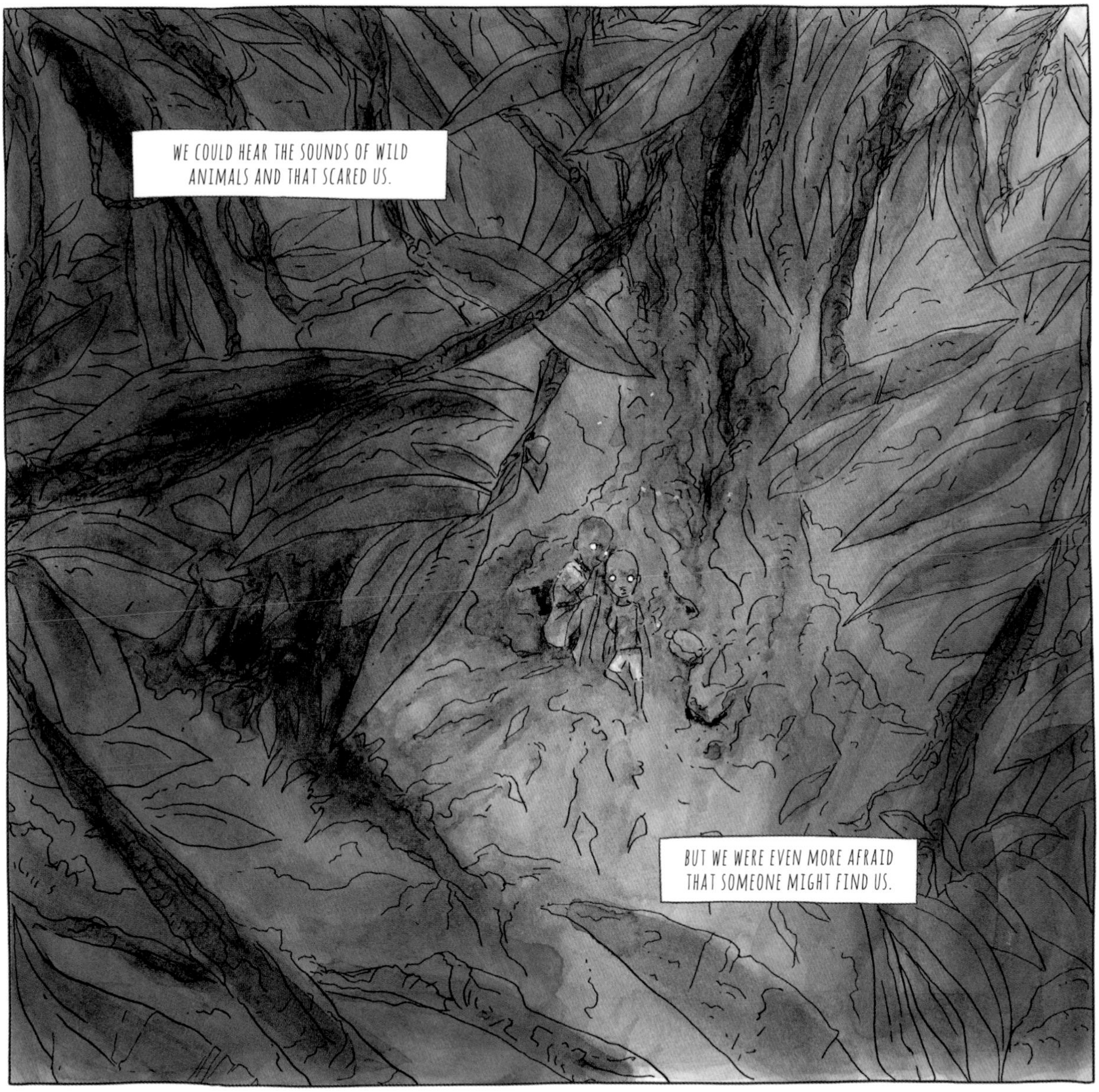

WE COULD HEAR THE SOUNDS OF WILD ANIMALS AND THAT SCARED US.

BUT WE WERE EVEN MORE AFRAID THAT SOMEONE MIGHT FIND US.

NO, WE CAN'T. WE HAVE ALMOST NO FOOD.

YES, HE NEEDS A REAL GROWNUP MAMA.

I HOPE SOMEONE FOUND HIM.

IF NO ONE DID, THEN HE DIED THERE UNDER THAT TREE...ALONE.

WE KEPT WALKING LIKE THAT FOR A FEW DAYS.
ALICE, I'M TIRED, I'M HUNGRY, AND WE HAVEN'T SEEN MAMA!
...

WAIT, STOP! I THINK THERE'S SOMEONE THERE! LET'S HIDE!

DO YOU THINK THEY AREN'T NICE PEOPLE?
SHH! NOT SO LOUD! I DON'T KNOW...

IT ISN'T MAMA, BUT I FEEL LIKE I KNOW THEM!
ME TOO!

IT LOOKS LIKE COUSIN DONATIEN!

BUT HE LOOKS REALLY SICK...
BUT WITH HIM, THERE'S...

AUNT ÉPIPHANIE!
WE'D MANAGED TO RUN INTO A DISTANT COUSIN ALONG WITH ONE OF OUR AUNTS.

WE WALKED AT NIGHT WITH THEM
AND HID DURING THE DAY TO SLEEP.
IT WAS MUCH SAFER FOR US.

BUT COUSIN DONATIEN
FELT WORSE AND WORSE.
WAIT! I CAN'T
KEEP GOING.
LEAVE ME HERE.

I'M GOING TO DIE
ANYHOW. YOU GO ON.

THEN HE LAID DOWN
AND WE WENT ON
WITH OUR AUNT.

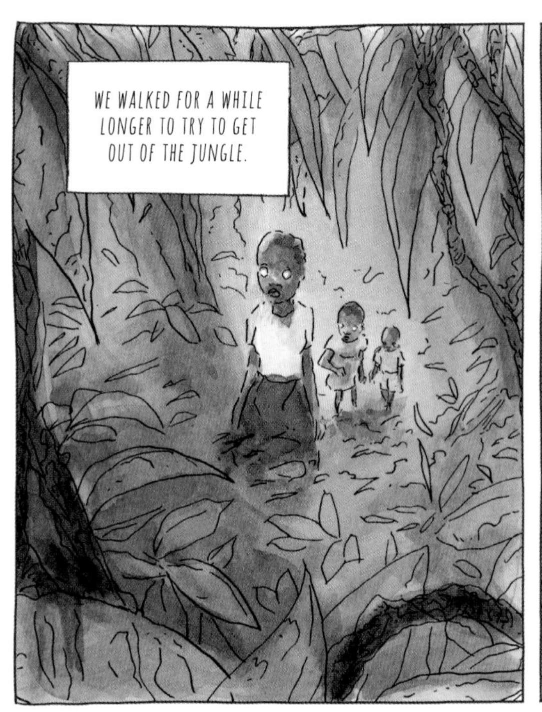
WE WALKED FOR A WHILE LONGER TO TRY TO GET OUT OF THE JUNGLE.

WE BEGAN TO SEE LIGHT...

...AND WE FOLLOWED IT...

...UNTIL WE FINALLY FOUND THE WAY OUT...

WE'D COME BACK ROUND TO OUR LAST CAMP...OR WHAT WAS LEFT OF IT.
WE'D PROBABLY BEEN IN THE JUNGLE FOR ABOUT TWO WEEKS.

WE HAD TO CROSS THE CAMP....

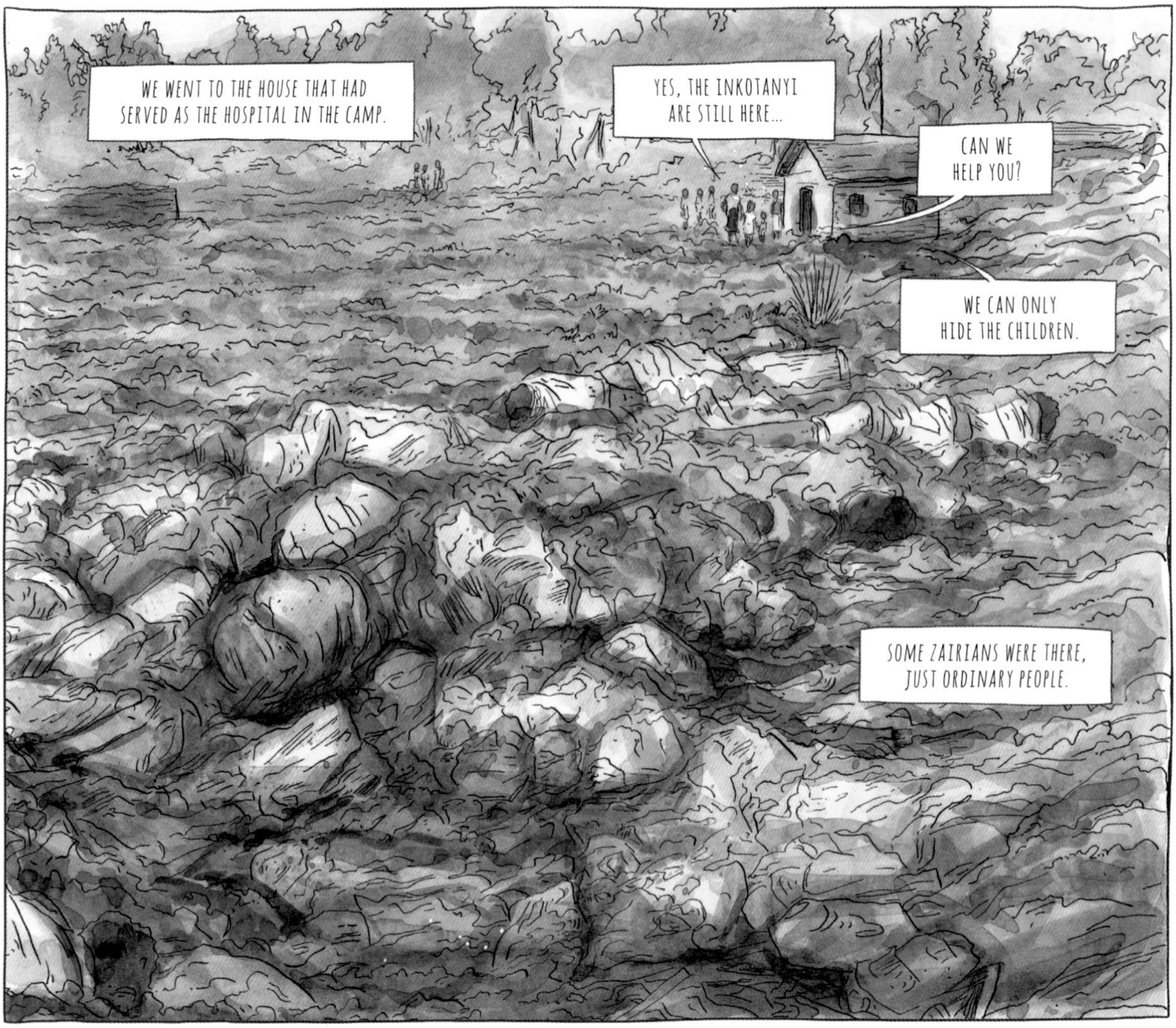

WE WENT TO THE HOUSE THAT HAD SERVED AS THE HOSPITAL IN THE CAMP.
YES, THE INKOTANYI ARE STILL HERE...
CAN WE HELP YOU?
WE CAN ONLY HIDE THE CHILDREN.
SOME ZAIRIANS WERE THERE, JUST ORDINARY PEOPLE.

IT WAS DANGEROUS FOR THEM TO HAVE US THERE. IT WAS AGAINST THE LAW TO HELP US.
DURING THE DAY, THEY HID US IN THE STY WITH THE PIGS.

BUT AT NIGHT, WE SLEPT IN THE HOUSE.

WE SPENT SEVERAL DAYS HIDDEN WITH THEM.

UNTIL ONE NIGHT, THEY CAME AND TOLD US WE HAD TO LEAVE.

SO WE LEFT WITHOUT REALLY KNOW-ING WHERE TO GO.
THERE WAS A YOUNG WOMAN WALKING BY HERSELF IN THE STREET, TOO.

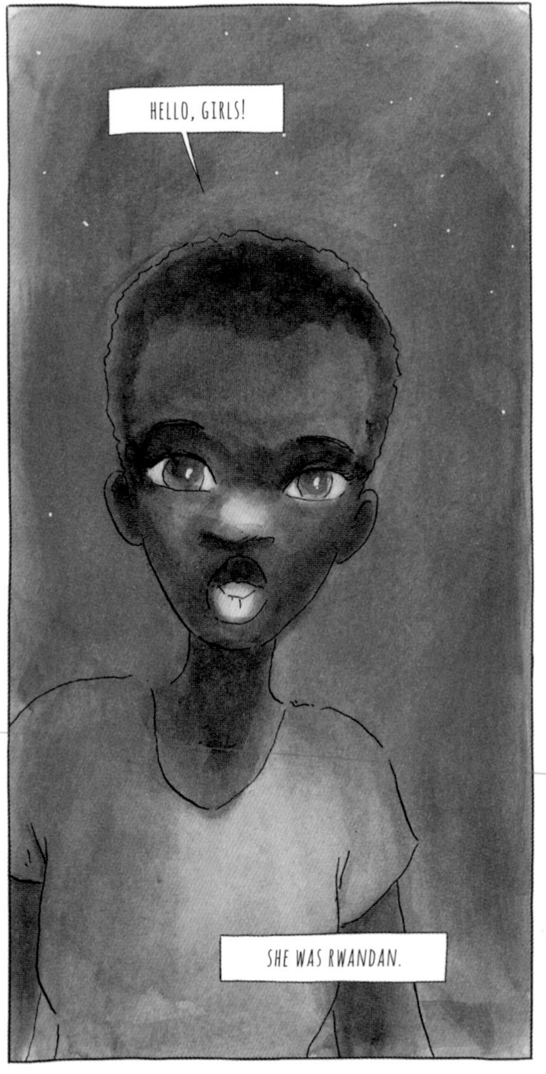
HELLO, GIRLS!
SHE WAS RWANDAN.

WHAT ARE YOUR NAMES?
ALICE.
ADELINE.

SHE TOOK US TO ANOTHER FAMILY, WHO LET US STAY WITH THEM.

YOU CAN SLEEP HERE.

THERE WERE ALREADY OTHER RWANDANS IN THE HOUSE...
...THREE YOUNG MEN...

WE DIDN'T KNOW THEM.
I JUST HOPED THEY WERE NICE...

THE YOUNG GIRL AND THE BOYS WORKED FOR THE FAMILY.

BUT THEY HID ADELINE AND ME.
HEY, ALICE, HOW LONG ARE WE STAYING HERE?
AND WILL WE SEE MAMA AGAIN SOON?

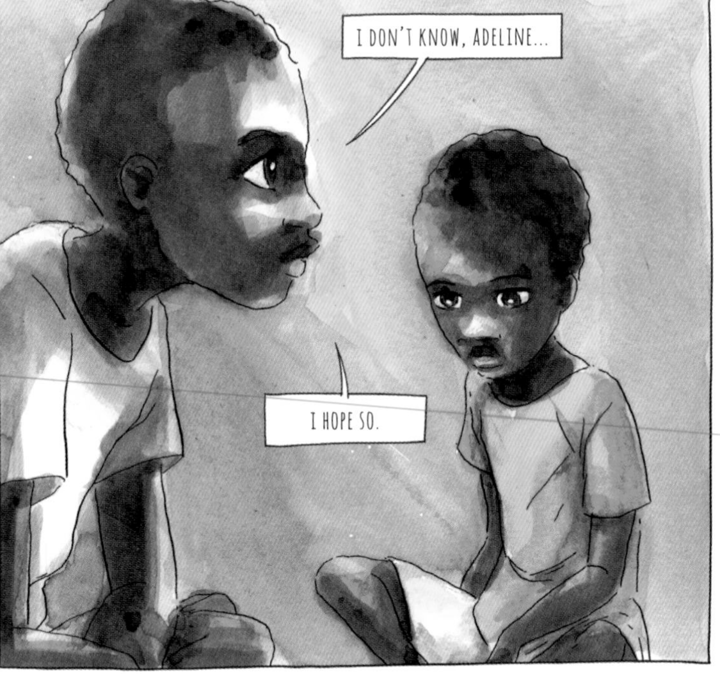
I DON'T KNOW, ADELINE...
I HOPE SO.

ONE NIGHT, THE YOUNG WOMAN WOKE US UP.
QUICK! GET UP! YOU HAVE TO LEAVE!

GO OUT THE LITTLE BACK WINDOW!
WE DID AS SHE SAID.

ONCE WE WERE OUTSIDE, WE HEARD THE YOUNG RWANDAN MEN TALKING TO THE GIRL.
WHERE ARE THEY?!
THEY'RE GONE! THEY'RE JUST CHILDREN!

LET ME DO THIS FOR THEM.

THAT NIGHT, THAT GIRL PROTECTED US FROM THOSE MEN.

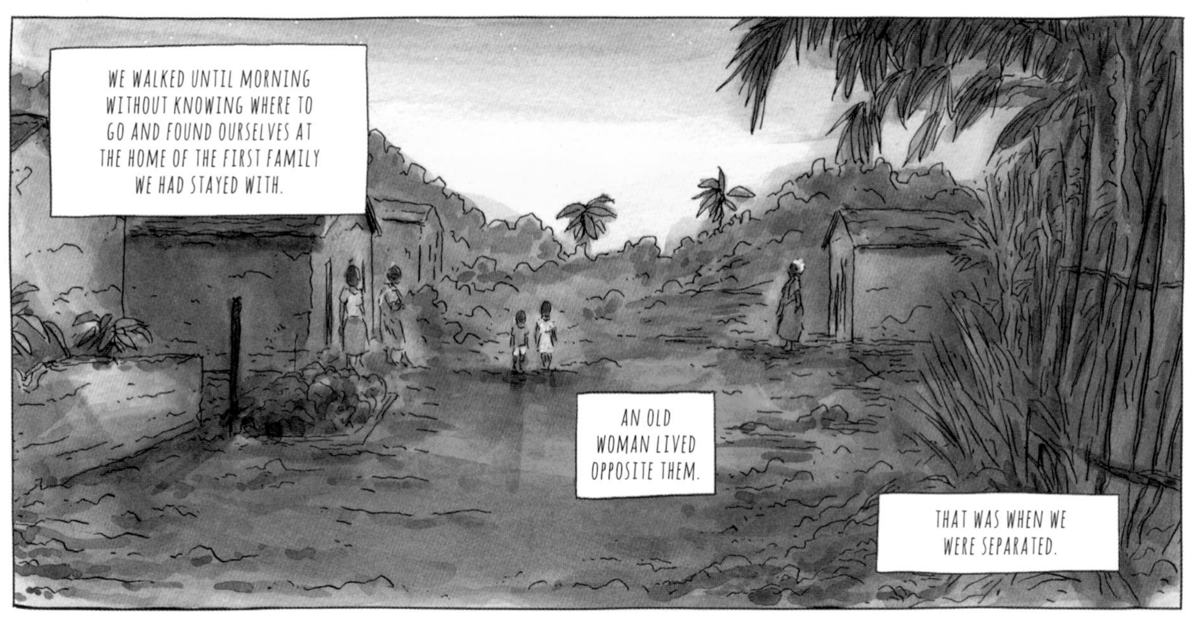
WE WALKED UNTIL MORNING WITHOUT KNOWING WHERE TO GO AND FOUND OURSELVES AT THE HOME OF THE FIRST FAMILY WE HAD STAYED WITH.
AN OLD WOMAN LIVED OPPOSITE THEM.
THAT WAS WHEN WE WERE SEPARATED.

I'LL TAKE CARE OF THE YOUNGER ONE.

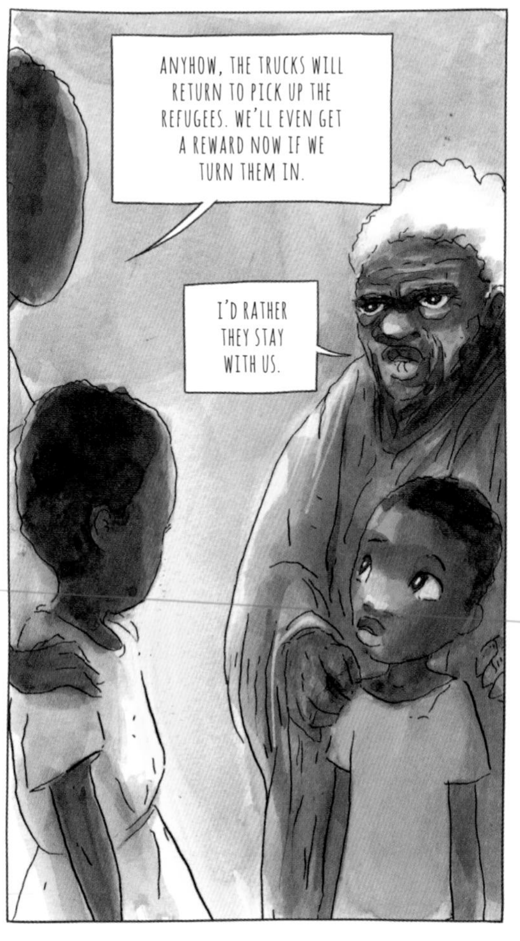
ANYHOW, THE TRUCKS WILL RETURN TO PICK UP THE REFUGEES. WE'LL EVEN GET A REWARD NOW IF WE TURN THEM IN.
I'D RATHER THEY STAY WITH US.

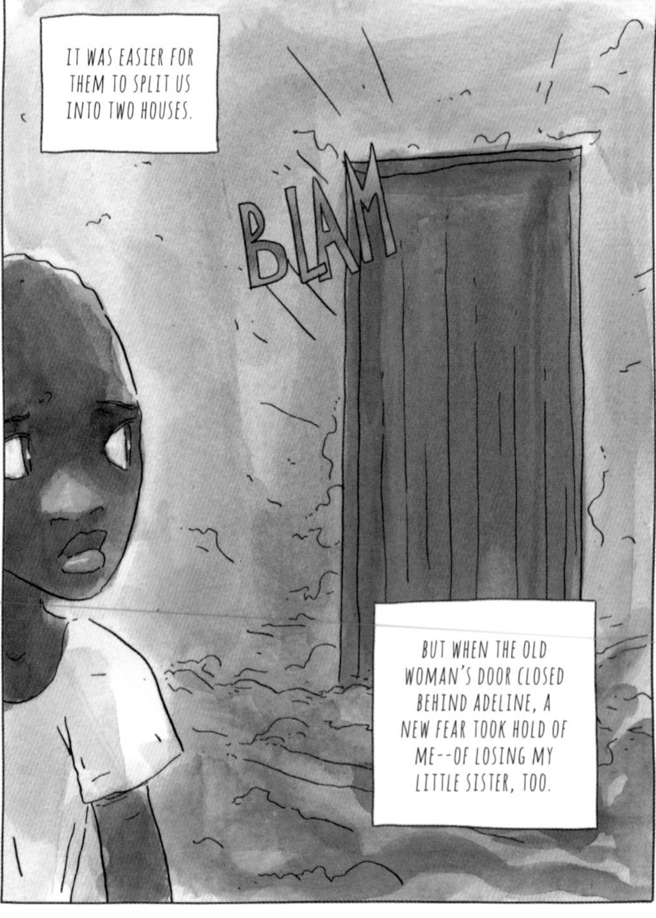
IT WAS EASIER FOR THEM TO SPLIT US INTO TWO HOUSES.
BLAM
BUT WHEN THE OLD WOMAN'S DOOR CLOSED BEHIND ADELINE, A NEW FEAR TOOK HOLD OF ME--OF LOSING MY LITTLE SISTER, TOO.

TWO DAYS LATER, A TRUCK STOPPED BY.
IT WAS THE ZAIRIANS PICKING UP REFUGEES.

I SAW THEM TALKING TO THE WOMAN I WAS STAYING WITH.
I THINK THEY GAVE HER SOME MONEY.

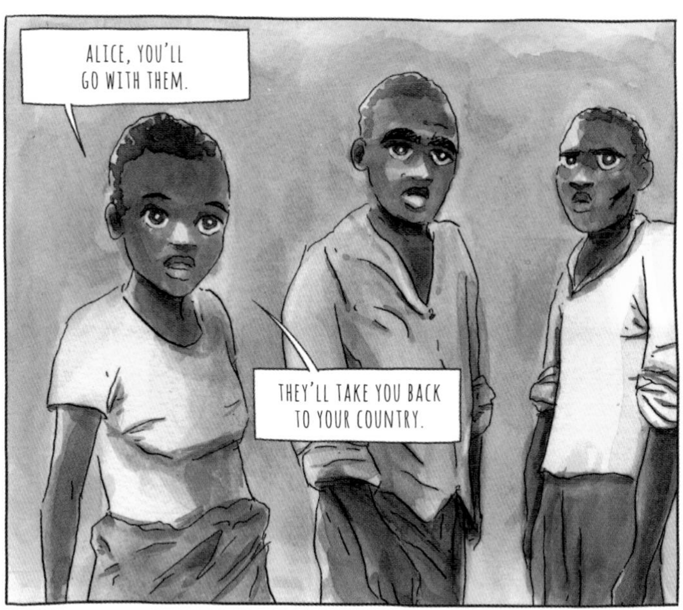
ALICE, YOU'LL GO WITH THEM.
THEY'LL TAKE YOU BACK TO YOUR COUNTRY.

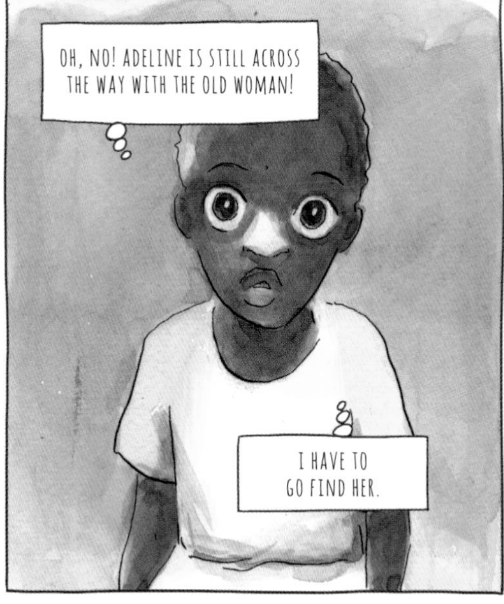
OH, NO! ADELINE IS STILL ACROSS THE WAY WITH THE OLD WOMAN!
I HAVE TO GO FIND HER.

I RAN TO THE OLD WOMAN'S HOUSE.

QUICK, QUICK! I HAVE TO GET ADELINE!

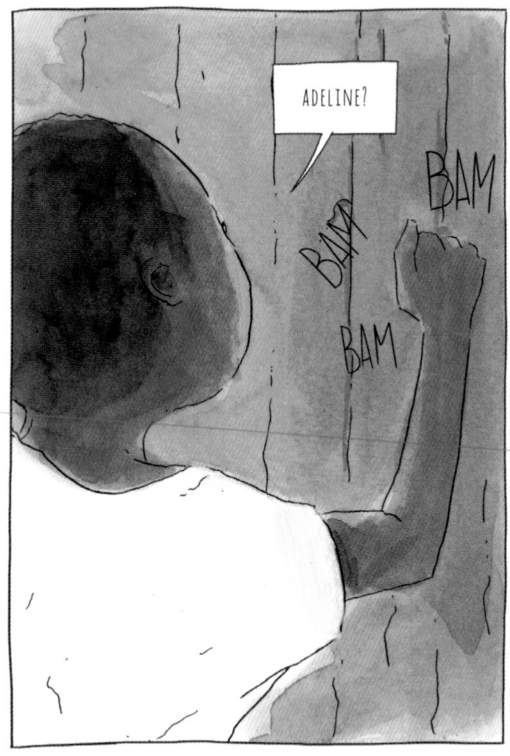

THE DOOR OPENED AND THE OLD WOMAN APPEARED.
WHAT'RE YOU DOING HERE? YOUR SISTER'S EATING... LEAVE HER. I'M TAKING CARE OF HER NOW. YOU'RE JUST A CHILD. HOW WILL YOU TAKE CARE OF HER?

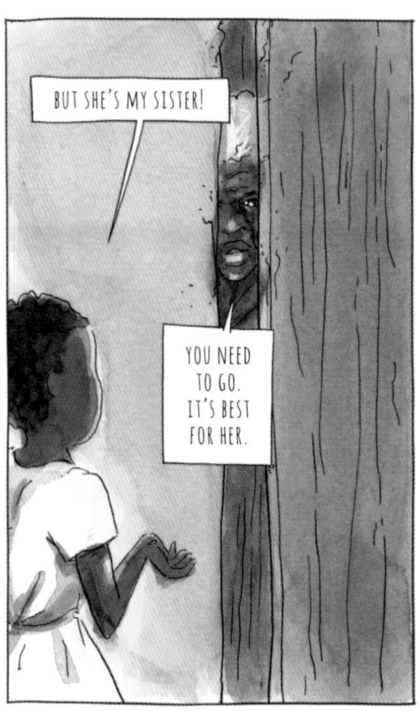

BUT SHE'S MY SISTER!
YOU NEED TO GO. IT'S BEST FOR HER.

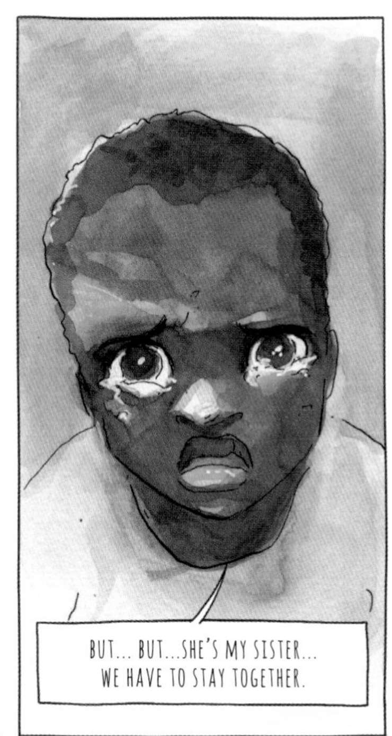

BUT... BUT...SHE'S MY SISTER... WE HAVE TO STAY TOGETHER.

ADELINE STAYED, AND I LEFT.

I THINK THE OLD WOMAN WANTED TO PROTECT HER BY KEEPING HER.

I HOPED SHE'D BE WELL LOOKED AFTER.

THE ZAIRIANS WHO TOOK ME WERE COLD, HARD MEN.
THEY DROVE PAST OUR LAST CAMP.

THEY DELIBERATELY STOPPED TO SHOW US THE CAMP CLEANUP.

THERE WERE PILES OF FULL SACKS EVERYWHERE.
ONE MAN SAID TO ME...
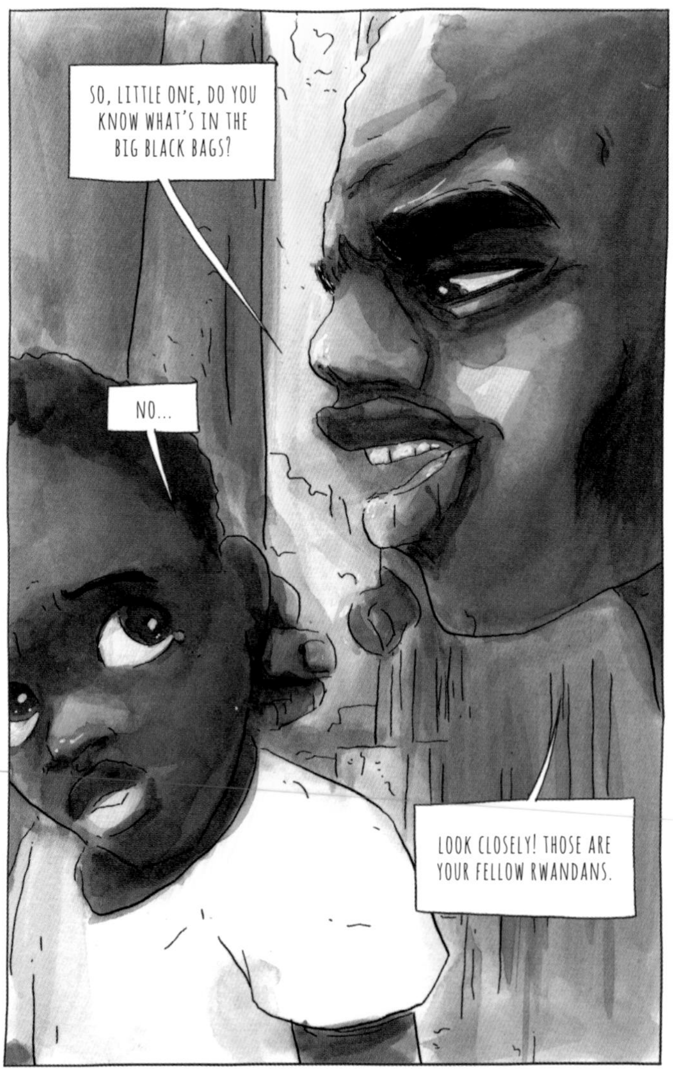
SO, LITTLE ONE, DO YOU KNOW WHAT'S IN THE BIG BLACK BAGS?
NO...
LOOK CLOSELY! THOSE ARE YOUR FELLOW RWANDANS.

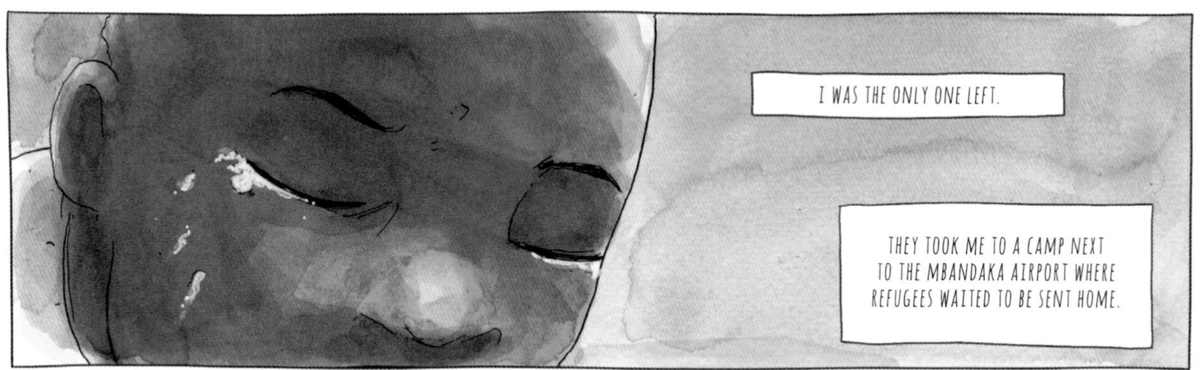

I WAS THE ONLY ONE LEFT.
THEY TOOK ME TO A CAMP NEXT TO THE MBANDAKA AIRPORT WHERE REFUGEES WAITED TO BE SENT HOME.

I WAS IN A BIG TENT FULL OF CHILDREN.
AT THAT MOMENT, I FELT TRULY LOST.

IT WAS AS IF I'D BECOME ANOTHER PERSON...

I STOOD, IN THE MIDST OF THE OTHER CHILDREN, STARING INTO SPACE.

I FELT DEAD INSIDE.

November 1997

MBANDAKA

Returning Home

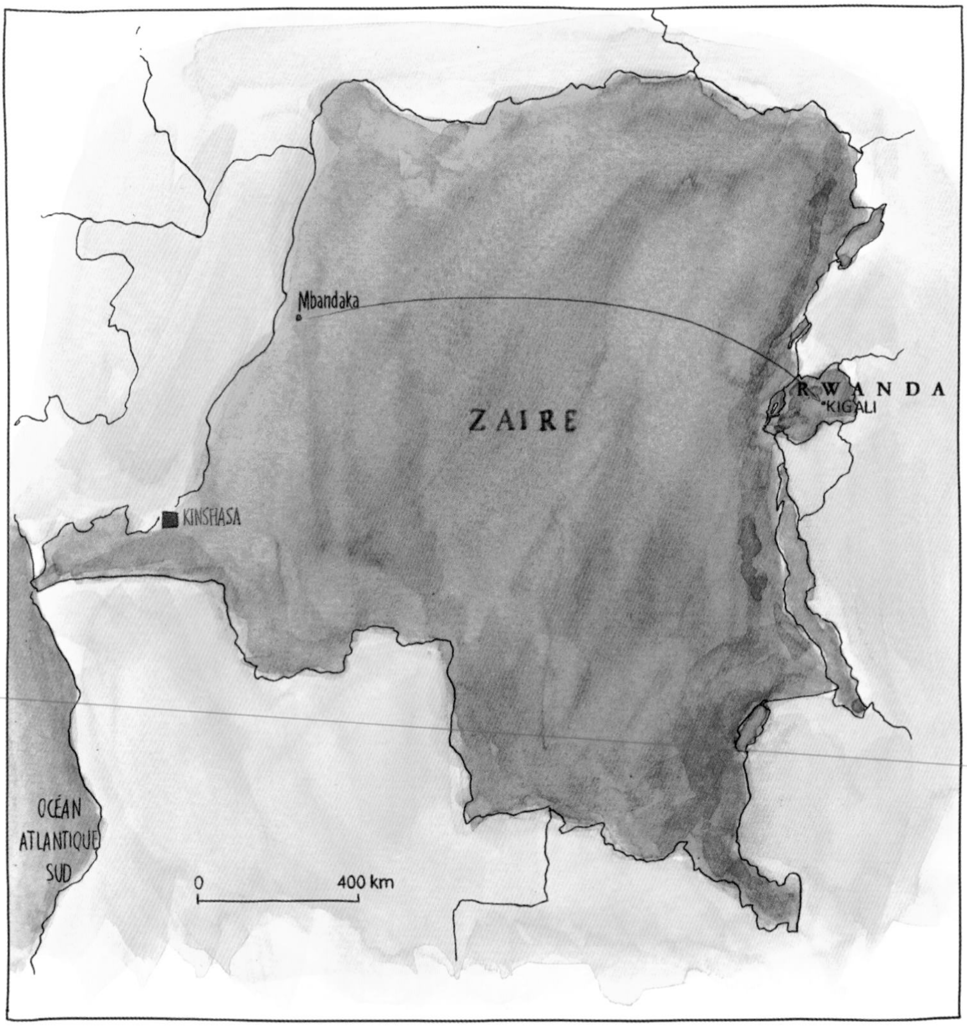

Mbandaka
RWANDA
KIGALI
ZAIRE
KINSHASA
OCÉAN ATLANTIQUE SUD
0
400 km

TWO DAYS LATER, THE OTHER CHILDREN AND I WERE CRAMMED INTO THE BACK OF A LITTLE WHITE AIRPLANE.
VRAOOM

THEY TOOK US TO AN ORPHANAGE IN KIGALI.
MY TIME THERE IS A HAZY MEMORY.

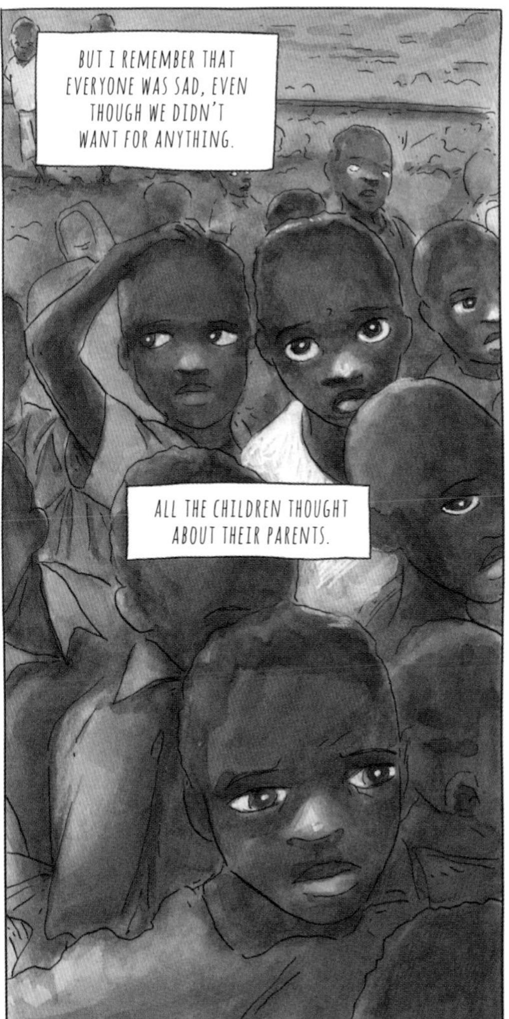
BUT I REMEMBER THAT EVERYONE WAS SAD, EVEN THOUGH WE DIDN'T WANT FOR ANYTHING.
ALL THE CHILDREN THOUGHT ABOUT THEIR PARENTS.

SOMETIMES I COULDN'T SLEEP FOR FEAR MY PARENTS WOULD COME TO FIND ME AND I WOULDN'T SEE THEM.

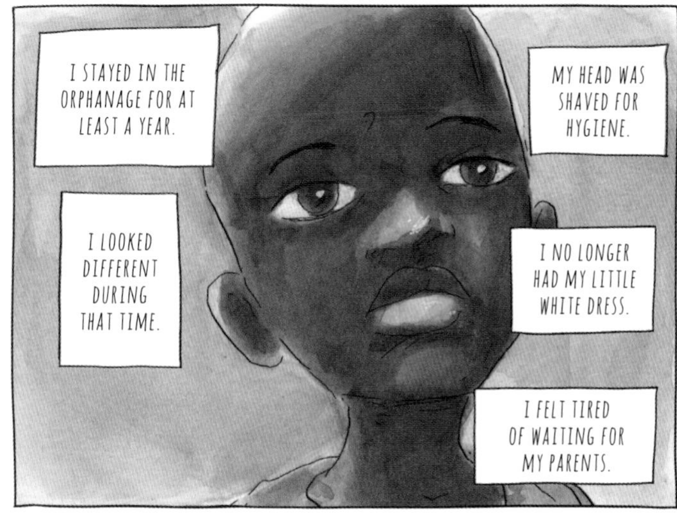
I STAYED IN THE ORPHANAGE FOR AT LEAST A YEAR.
MY HEAD WAS SHAVED FOR HYGIENE.
I LOOKED DIFFERENT DURING THAT TIME.
I NO LONGER HAD MY LITTLE WHITE DRESS.
I FELT TIRED OF WAITING FOR MY PARENTS.

AFTER A WHILE, WHEN I WAS ALMOST TEN YEARS OLD, THE WOMAN WHO WAS TAKING CARE OF US CAME LOOKING FOR ME.

ALICE, I NEED TO SPEAK TO YOU!

WHAT IS IT?

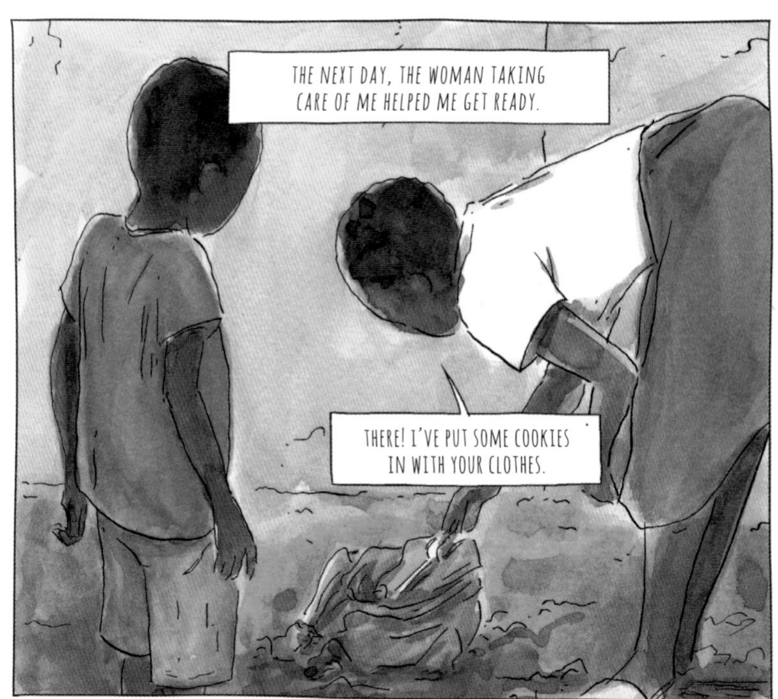
THE NEXT DAY, THE WOMAN TAKING CARE OF ME HELPED ME GET READY.
THERE! I'VE PUT SOME COOKIES IN WITH YOUR CLOTHES.

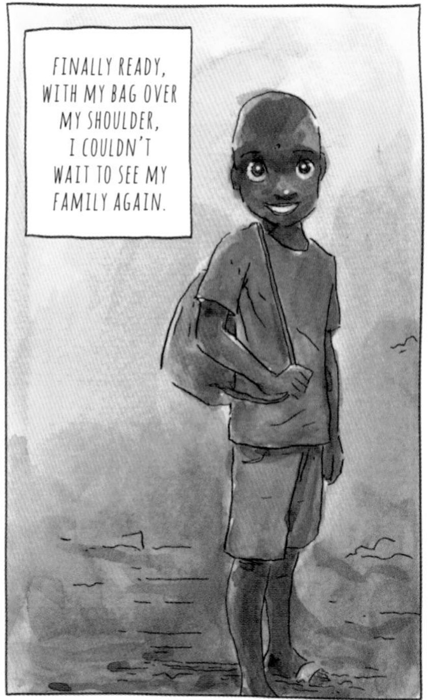
FINALLY READY, WITH MY BAG OVER MY SHOULDER, I COULDN'T WAIT TO SEE MY FAMILY AGAIN.

I GOT INTO A CAR WITH OTHER CHILDREN WHO CAME FROM THE SAME AREA AND WE LEFT.
I WAS ALREADY IMAGINING MY MOTHER AND SISTER. I WAS SO HAPPY.

BUT I KNEW ADELINE WOULDN'T BE THERE...
...AND I WAS A LITTLE SCARED ABOUT TELLING MAMA WHERE I'D LEFT HER.

January 1998

NEAR GITARAMA

COMING HOME...

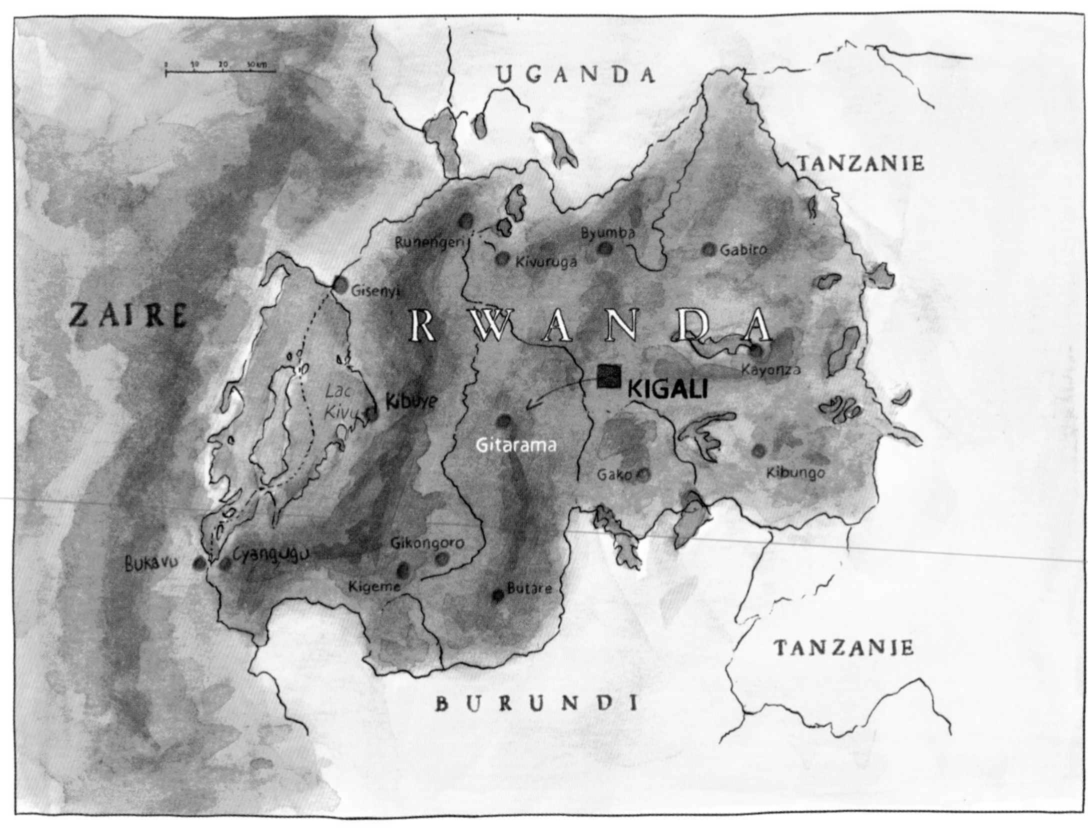

WE WENT TO A MARKET NEAR GITARAMA, NOT FAR FROM MY HOUSE.

ALICE

THEY GAVE US A CARD WITH OUR NAME ON IT SO WE'D BE RECOGNIZED.

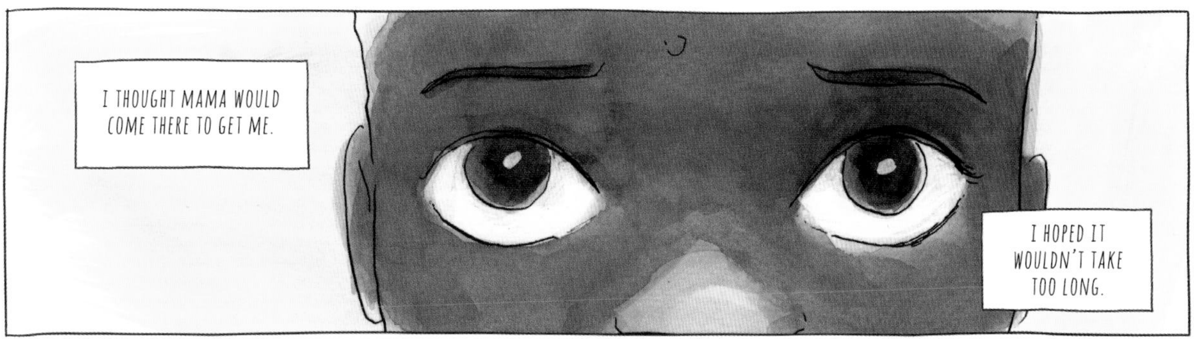

I THOUGHT MAMA WOULD COME THERE TO GET ME.
I HOPED IT WOULDN'T TAKE TOO LONG.

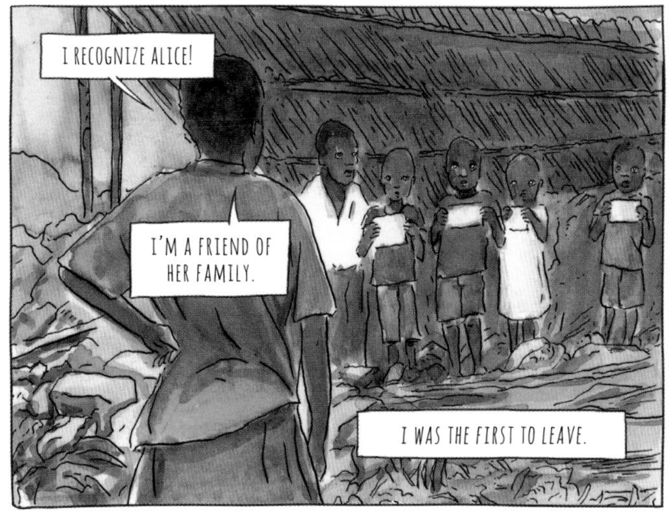

I RECOGNIZE ALICE!
I'M A FRIEND OF HER FAMILY.
I WAS THE FIRST TO LEAVE.

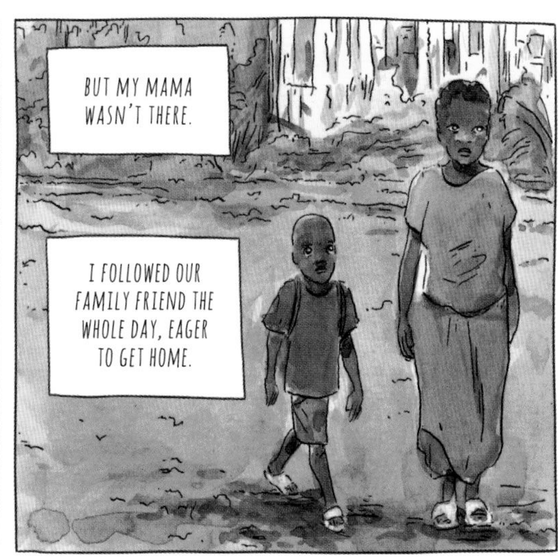

BUT MY MAMA WASN'T THERE.
I FOLLOWED OUR FAMILY FRIEND THE WHOLE DAY, EAGER TO GET HOME.

THAT EVENING, WE REACHED MY UNCLE FRANÇOIS' HOUSE.

HIS HOUSE WAS IN THE SAME VILLAGE AS MY PARENTS'.

BUT I STILL HADN'T SEEN MY MAMA.
AND I WAS SLEEPY...

IT WAS LATE. SO I LAY DOWN, TELLING MYSELF I'D PROBABLY SEE HER THE NEXT DAY.

I WOKE UP LATE IN THE MORNING. I WAS LOOKING FORWARD TO SEEING MAMA.
I ALSO KNEW THAT MY UNCLE HAD A SON I COULD PLAY WITH.

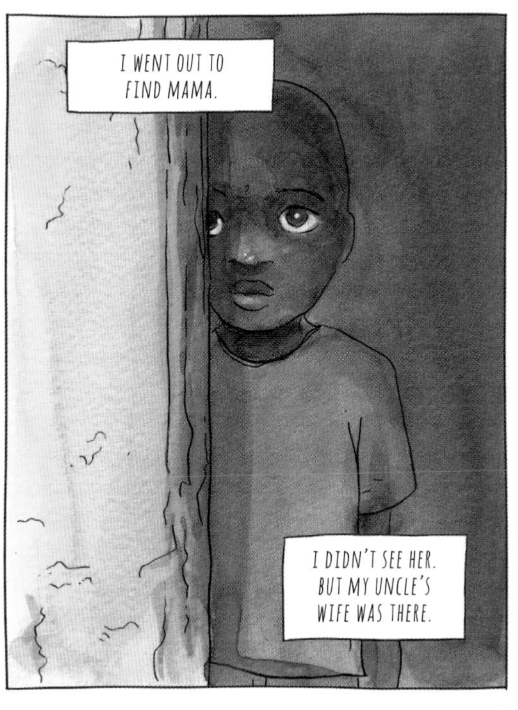
I WENT OUT TO FIND MAMA.
I DIDN'T SEE HER. BUT MY UNCLE'S WIFE WAS THERE.

THERE YOU ARE. DO YOU WANT SOMETHING TO EAT?
NO, I'M NOT HUNGRY.
WHERE'S MAMA?

I DON'T KNOW. SHE DIDN'T COME BACK.
...

YOUR PARENTS PROBA-BLY DIED WHEN THEY FLED TO ZAIRE, LIKE OUR SON.
GO SEE YOUR OLD HOUSE. IT'S AT THE END OF THE ROAD. YOU'LL UNDERSTAND.

SO I WENT TO THE END OF THE ROAD AND SAW OUR OLD HOUSE WITHOUT RECOGNIZING IT.
IT WAS A WRECK. NOBODY LIVED THERE ANYMORE.

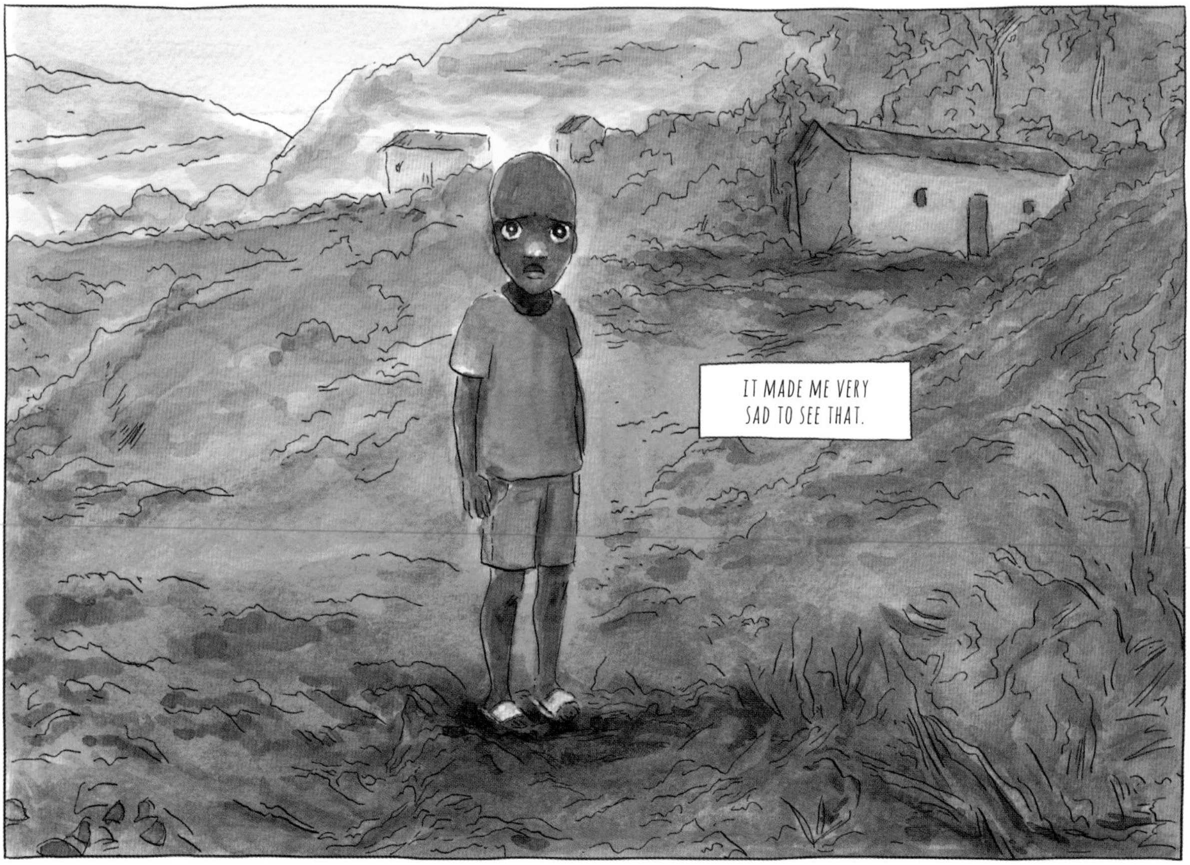

IT MADE ME VERY SAD TO SEE THAT.

FROM THAT DAY ON,
I WAS TRULY ALONE.
MY UNCLE AND HIS WIFE
WERE GONE EVERY DAY,
LEAVING ME ALONE OUTSIDE
THEIR LOCKED DOOR.

I'D SIT THERE THE WHOLE TIME WITH NOTHING TO DO.

SOMETIMES I EVEN FELL ASLEEP IN BROAD DAYLIGHT IN FRONT OF THAT DOOR.

AT MY UNCLE FRANÇOIS' HOUSE, MY CHORE WAS TO GO GET WATER.

IT WAS ALL THE WAY DOWN AT THE BOTTOM OF THE HILL.
AT FIRST, I COULD ONLY CARRY TWO GALLONS.
CARRYING A TWO-GALLON CONTAINER WHEN YOU'RE NINE YEARS OLD ISN'T EASY.

AFTER A FEW MONTHS, I COULD CARRY A FOUR-GALLON CONTAINER.
I FELT LIKE IT WAS SQUASHING MY NECK. IT WAS HARD TO BREATHE, BUT I GOT USED TO IT.

THAT'S WHAT MY LIFE WAS LIKE FOR ALMOST A YEAR.

SEVERAL MONTHS LATER, AUNT MÉDIATRICE, ONE OF UNCLE FRANÇOIS' SISTERS, RETURNED TO THE VILLAGE.

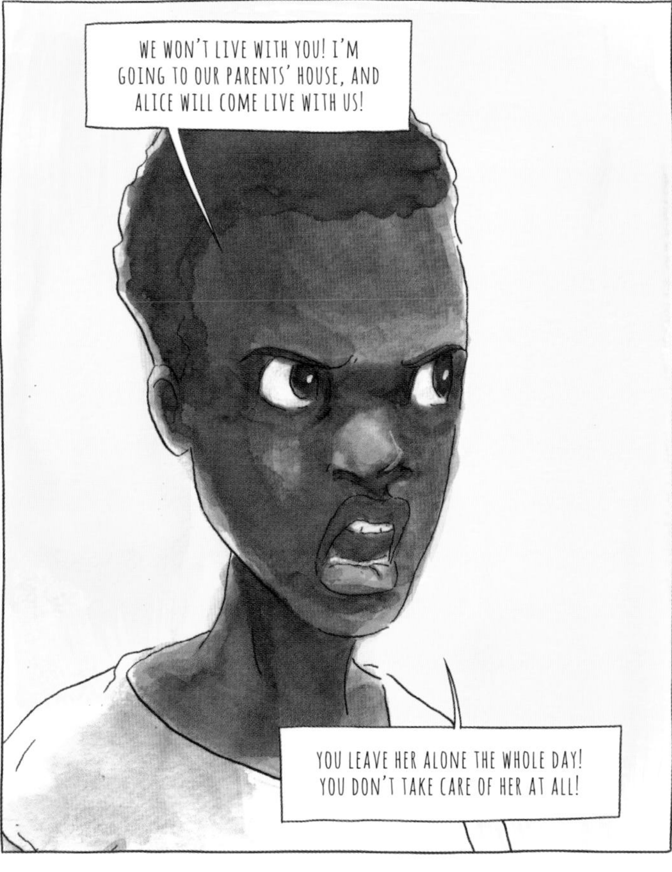

WE WON'T LIVE WITH YOU! I'M GOING TO OUR PARENTS' HOUSE, AND ALICE WILL COME LIVE WITH US!
YOU LEAVE HER ALONE THE WHOLE DAY! YOU DON'T TAKE CARE OF HER AT ALL!

ABSOLUTELY NOT! ALICE STAYS HERE!
YOU CAN LEAVE IF YOU WANT, BUT I'M KEEPING THE LAND!

MY UNCLE FRANÇOIS GAVE AUNT MÉDIATRICE ONLY TWO FIELDS.
SO SHE FILED A COMPLAINT AND ENDED UP WITH HER SHARE OF THE LAND.

MY UNCLE KEPT MY PARENTS' LAND BECAUSE HE WAS THE ONE PAYING TO FEED ME.

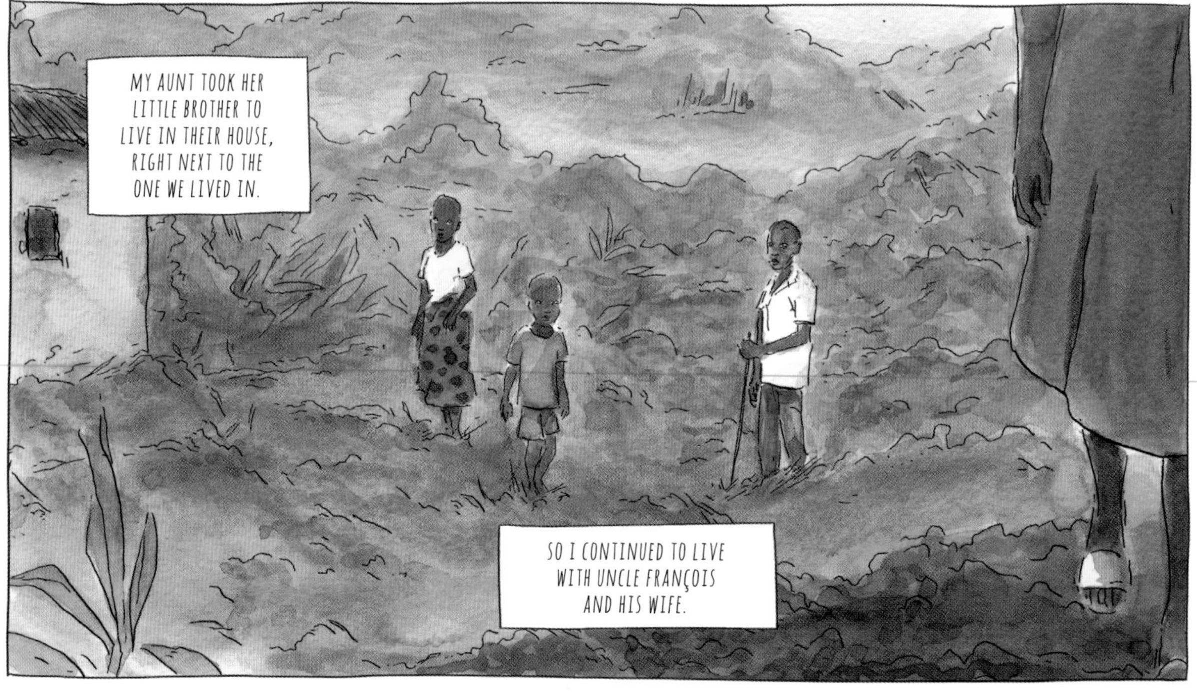
MY AUNT TOOK HER LITTLE BROTHER TO LIVE IN THEIR HOUSE, RIGHT NEXT TO THE ONE WE LIVED IN.
SO I CONTINUED TO LIVE WITH UNCLE FRANÇOIS AND HIS WIFE.

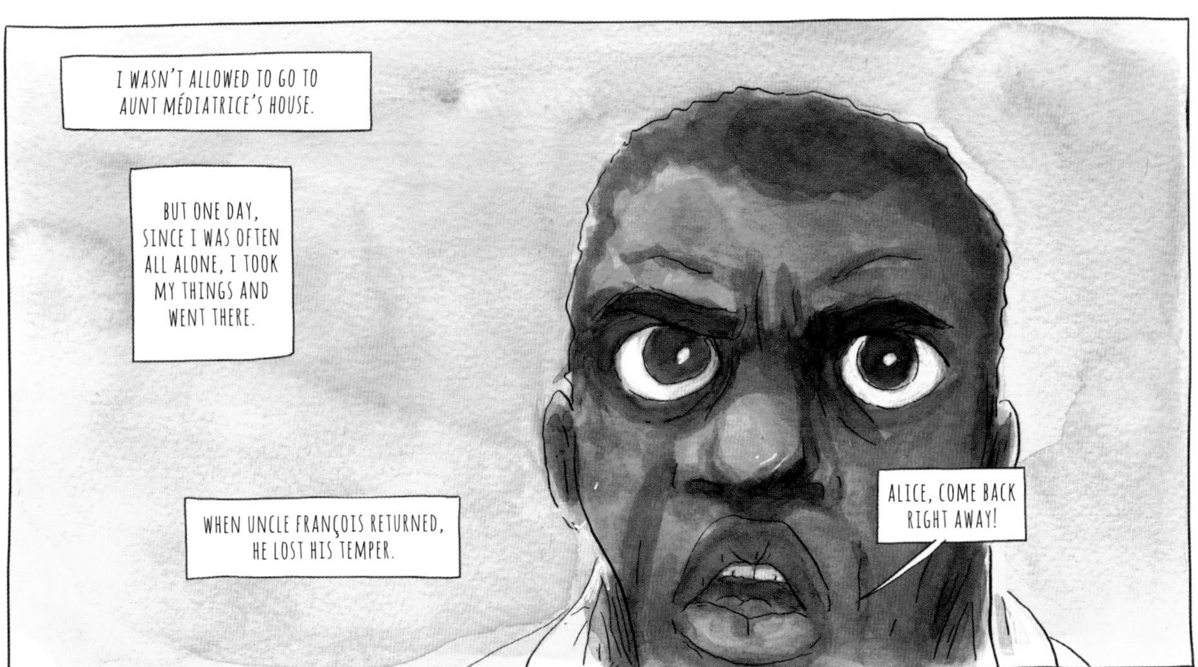
I WASN'T ALLOWED TO GO TO AUNT MÉDIATRICE'S HOUSE.
BUT ONE DAY, SINCE I WAS OFTEN ALL ALONE, I TOOK MY THINGS AND WENT THERE.
WHEN UNCLE FRANÇOIS RETURNED, HE LOST HIS TEMPER.
ALICE, COME BACK RIGHT AWAY!

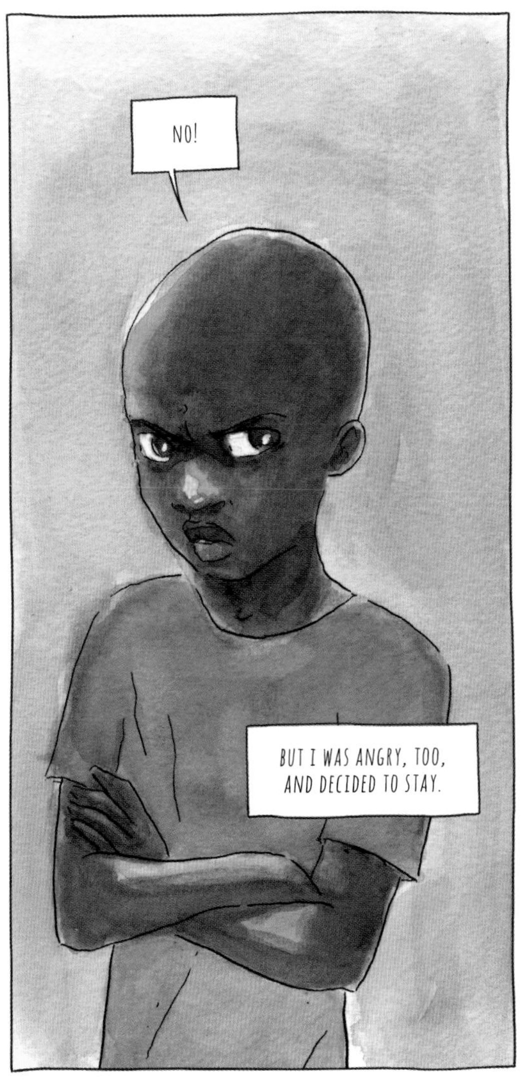
NO!
BUT I WAS ANGRY, TOO, AND DECIDED TO STAY.

SO MY UNCLE GRABBED A STICK...
ALICE, DON'T MAKE ME COME GET YOU!

ALICE, COME HERE NOW OR ELSE I'M GOING TO GET ANGRY.
...AND HE CAME TO GET ME.

QUICK! GET INSIDE!
BUT WE QUICKLY WENT BACK INSIDE MY AUNT'S HOUSE.

BLAM!
AND BETWEEN US, WE MANAGED TO KEEP THE DOOR CLOSED.

OPEN THE DOOR!
NO, I'VE LEFT AND I WON'T GO BACK TO YOUR HOUSE!

MY UNCLE ENDED UP GOING BACK TO HIS HOUSE. SEEING HOW DETERMINED I WAS, HE AGREED TO LET ME LIVE AT AUNT MÉDIATRICE'S HOUSE. I THINK MY UNCLE WASN'T A BAD PERSON DEEP DOWN.

WHEN I MOVED INTO MY AUNT'S HOUSE, I'D ALREADY BEEN COUGHING FOR A DAY OR TWO.

THEN IT GOT WORSE...

I STARTED TO RUN A FEVER AND MY SIDES HURT WHEN I BREATHED.

I COUGHED MORE AND MORE.
AND MY NECK ACHED SO MUCH I COULDN'T TURN MY HEAD TO THE SIDE ANYMORE.

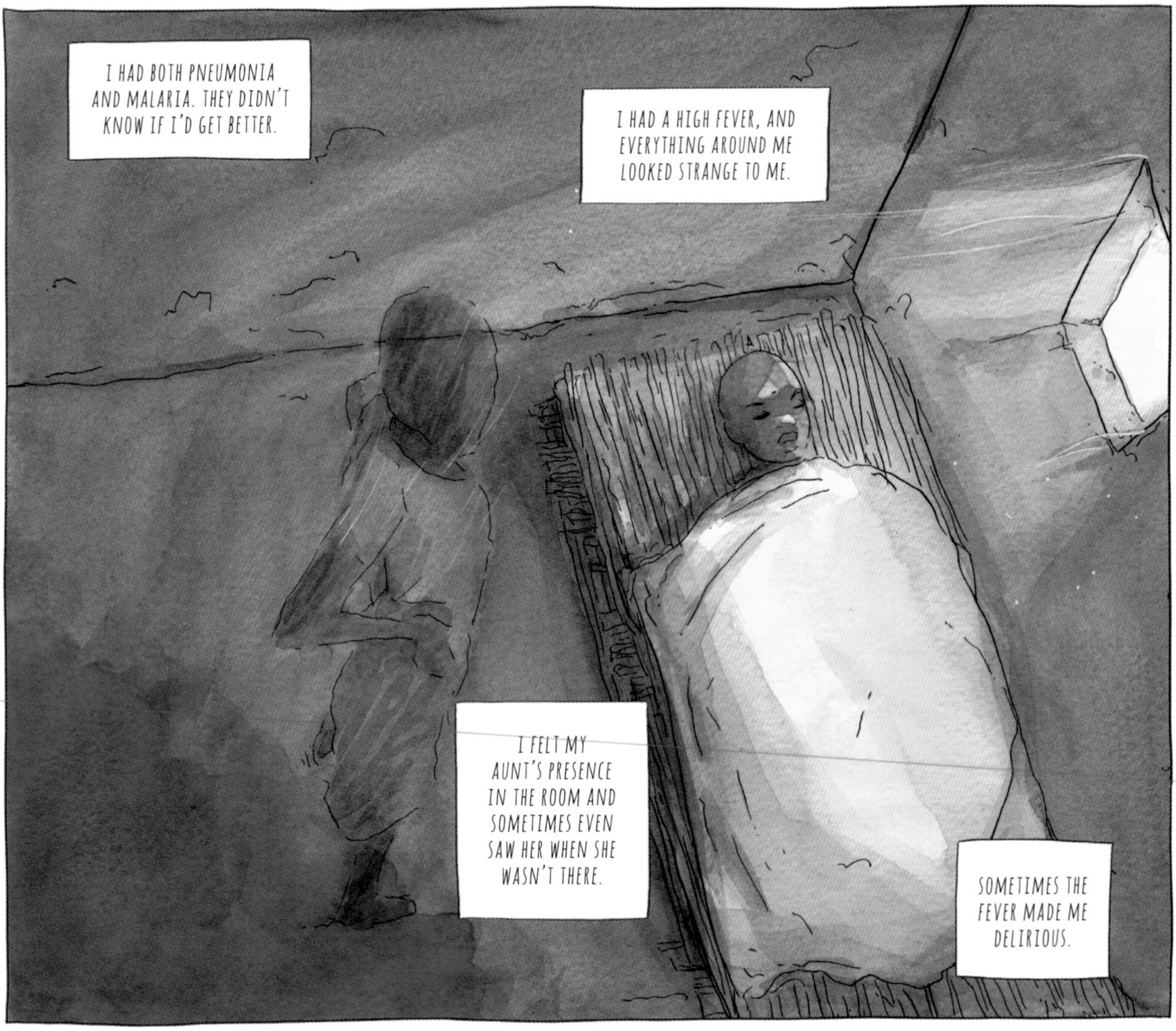

I HAD BOTH PNEUMONIA AND MALARIA. THEY DIDN'T KNOW IF I'D GET BETTER.

I HAD A HIGH FEVER, AND EVERYTHING AROUND ME LOOKED STRANGE TO ME.

I FELT MY AUNT'S PRESENCE IN THE ROOM AND SOMETIMES EVEN SAW HER WHEN SHE WASN'T THERE.

SOMETIMES THE FEVER MADE ME DELIRIOUS.

MY AUNT WENT TO ASK THE PRIEST FOR HELP.

HE GAVE HER SOME MONEY.

SHE WAS ABLE TO TAKE ME TO THE HOSPITAL.

THEY TOOK CARE OF ME RIGHT AWAY.

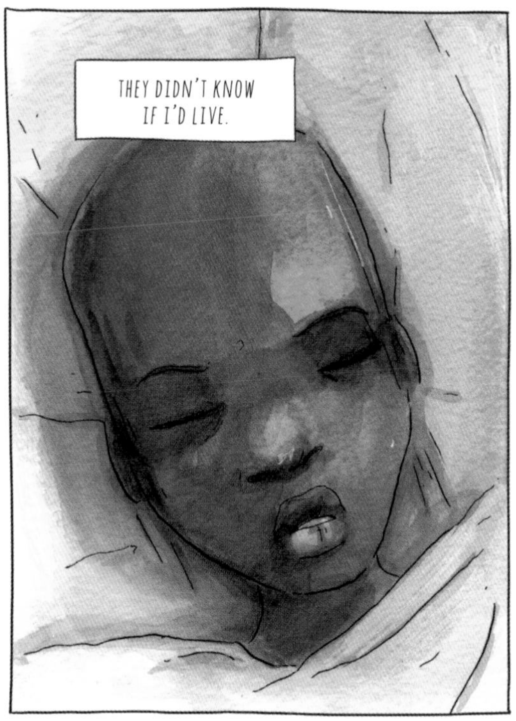
THEY DIDN'T KNOW IF I'D LIVE.

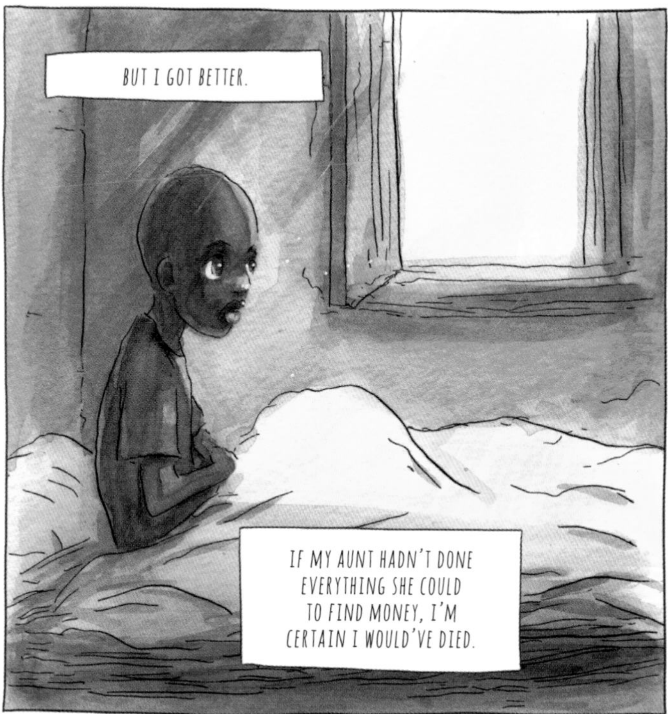
BUT I GOT BETTER.
IF MY AUNT HADN'T DONE EVERYTHING SHE COULD TO FIND MONEY, I'M CERTAIN I WOULD'VE DIED.

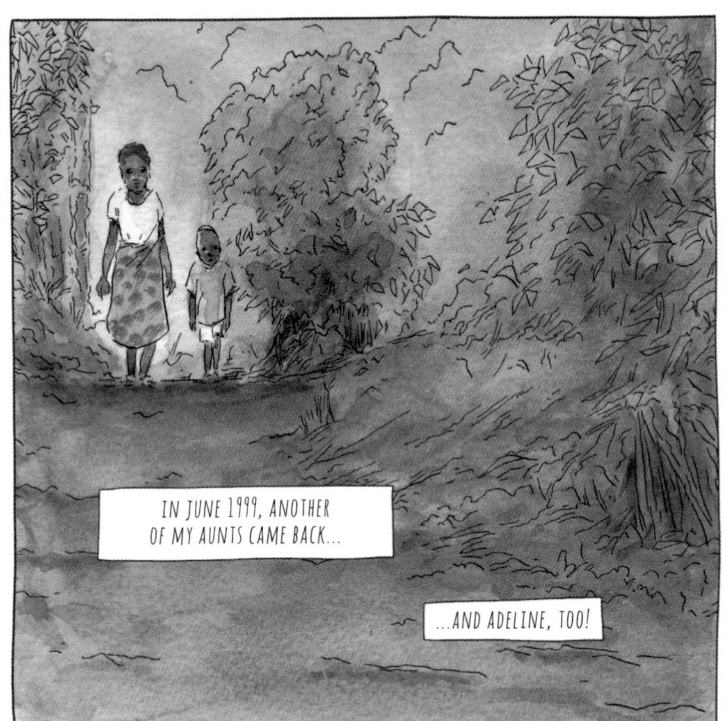

IN JUNE 1999, ANOTHER OF MY AUNTS CAME BACK...
...AND ADELINE, TOO!

I'M SO GLAD YOU'RE HERE!
WHERE'VE YOU BEEN ALL THIS TIME?
I'M GLAD TO BE HERE TOO.
AT THE ORPHANAGE.

WE WERE FINALLY TOGETHER.

WHY ISN'T MAMA HERE?

I DON'T KNOW, ADELINE.

ADELINE WAS ALSO DISAPPOINTED THAT MAMA WASN'T THERE.

DO YOU THINK MAMA ABANDONED US?
NO, I DON'T THINK SO.
WE MISSED OUR MAMA.

BUT OUR AUNTS DID EVERYTHING FOR US TO BE COMFORTABLE.
OH, THERE YOU ARE! LOOK WHAT I'VE BROUGHT.
THEY GAVE US COOKIES AND CAKES THEY'D BOUGHT.

YOU COULD SAY OUR LIVES HAD ALMOST BECOME NORMAL AGAIN.
THEN WE GOT NEWS THAT CHANGED THEM AGAIN.

ONE DAY IN JULY 2000...
I HAVE SOMETHING TO TELL YOU.

WE'VE JUST FOUND OUT WHAT HAPPENED TO YOUR SISTER ALINE AND YOUR PARENTS.

THEY'RE ALIVE, AND THEY'RE IN BELGIUM.
YOU'LL BE ABLE TO BE WITH THEM.

December 2001

KENYA

LEAVING

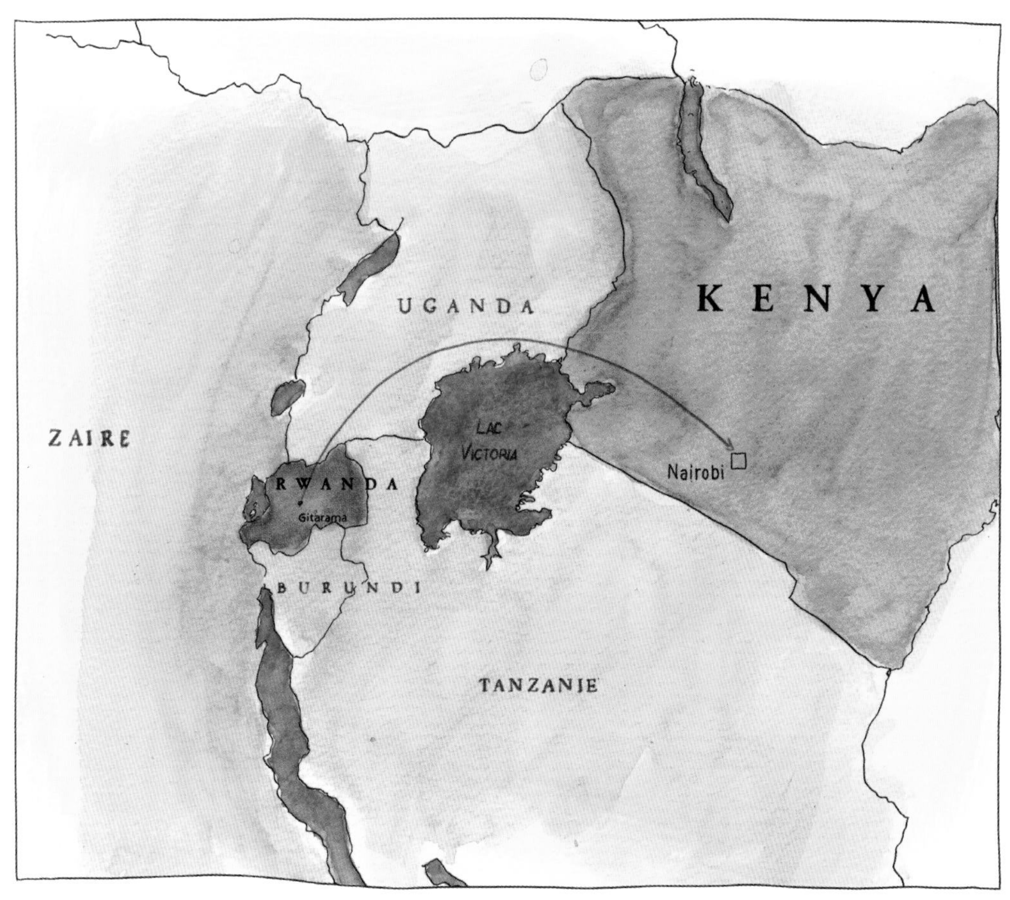

BELGIUM HAD AGREED TO LET US JOIN OUR FAMILY. BUT RWANDA REFUSED TO LET US LEAVE.

THAT'S WHY WE DECIDED TO GO TO KENYA TO CATCH A PLANE.

IT WAS THE LAST TIME I SAW MY COUNTRY.

ADELINE AND I LEFT RWANDA ON A BUS, ACCOMPANIED BY A NEIGHBOR WHO WAS ALSO GOING TO KENYA WITH HER CHILDREN.

WE ARRIVED IN KENYA AT THE END OF 2001.

MY PARENTS HAD DIFFICULTY GETTING THE PAPERS WE NEEDED FOR OUR JOURNEY.
WHILE WE WAITED, WE LIVED IN A LITTLE HOUSE NEAR NAIROBI.

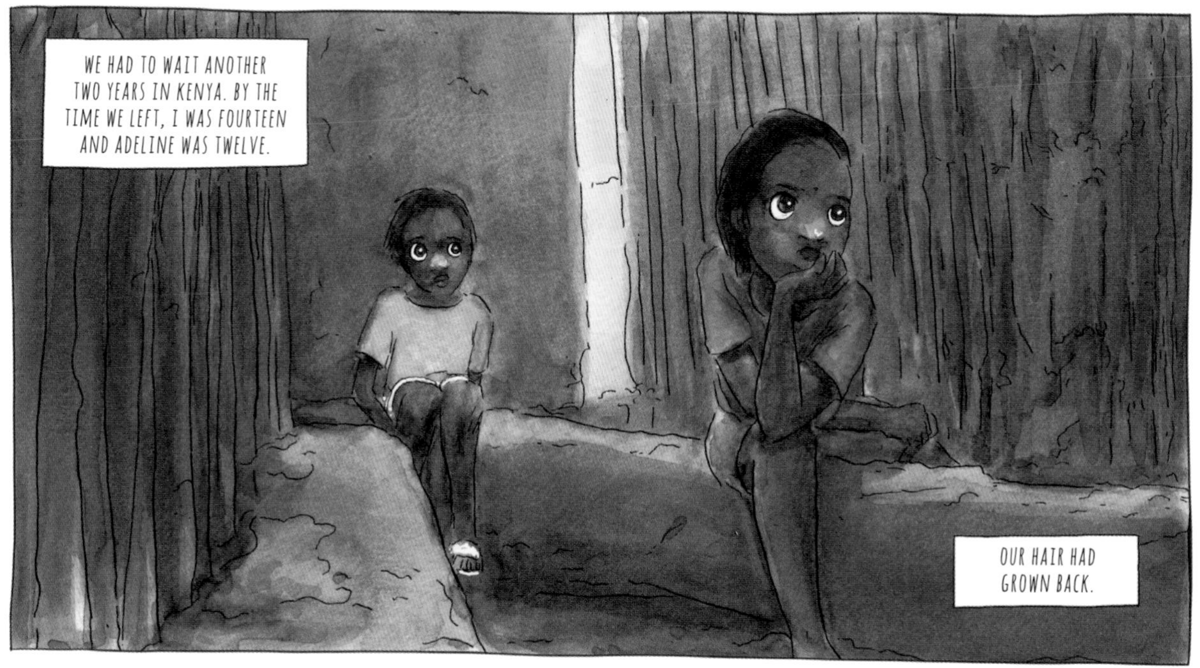
WE HAD TO WAIT ANOTHER TWO YEARS IN KENYA. BY THE TIME WE LEFT, I WAS FOURTEEN AND ADELINE WAS TWELVE.
OUR HAIR HAD GROWN BACK.

NAIROBI AIRPORT, KENYA.

ALICE, WILL YOU RECOGNIZE THEM AFTER ALL THIS TIME?

December 2003

BRUSSELS

Landing

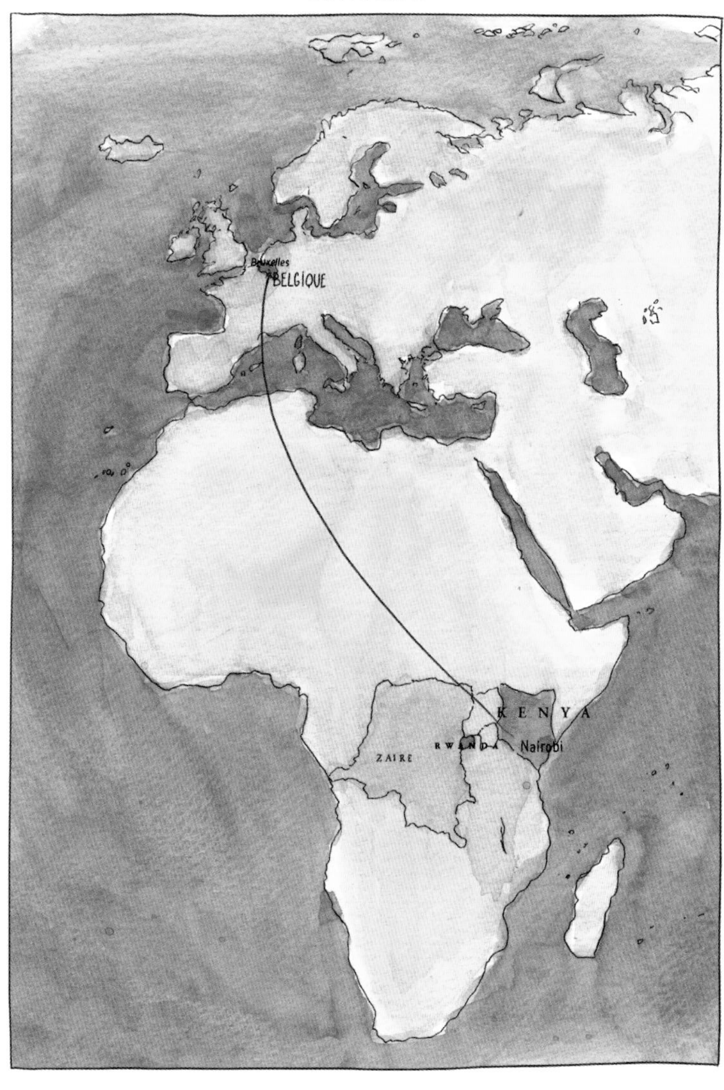

WE ARRIVED IN BRUSSELS AROUND 6 A.M. IT WAS STILL NIGHT AND VERY COLD.
AN ESCORT TOOK US TO THE ARRIVAL HALL.

THERE ARE YOUR PARENTS.

I SAW MY MAMA.
SHE WAS WITH ALINE, MY FATHER, A NEW LITTLE BROTHER AND A NEW LITTLE SISTER.

SHE STARTED CRYING AS SHE WAS TALKING TO US.

MY LITTLE GIRLS HAVE BECOME YOUNG LADIES!

AND SO...

...EVEN THOUGH I COULD HARDLY BELIEVE IT, WE WERE FINALLY BACK WITH MAMA!

AND THAT MADE ME HAPPY.

ALICE ON THE RUN
FROM THE EYES OF AN ADULT

During her flight, Alice was still a child. Gaspard Talmasse has chosen to tell her odyssey—her flight—by respecting her viewpoint as a child, showing only what she remembered and what she noticed. In addition, we thought it would be worth having an adult's perspective of all these events. Alice's mother agreed to answer our questions.

Could you tell us about your flight from Rwanda in a few words? Why did you leave? Who was Rose, the child you took with you?

Hatred towards the Tutsis had been growing for some time, little by little. We thought it would end by becoming a pogrom, as had happened during the 1960s. But in 1994, following the attack that killed the Rwandan and Burundi presidents, that hate turned into genocide. We never thought it would go that far.

When it began, Tutsi families scattered, hiding themselves in the homes of their Hutu friends. I was teaching French at the village school. Rose, one of my students, came to my house to ask for help. We took her in and hid her.

When the RPF took control of the country, we heard that their soldiers left many dead Hutus in their wake. Therefore, we decided to flee. Rose came with us.

There were Interhamwe roadblocks throughout the country. My husband strongly resembles a Tutsi. That's why, despite having papers that listed our ethnicity, the militias at one of the checkpoints made my husband and me lay down on the ground. We truly thought they were going to kill us. But one of them recognized us and let us pass. The children were in a truck and weren't aware of anything.

Some Interhamwe threatened the people in the camps who looked like Tutsis. They even killed some of them. Rose decided to take her chances in Rwanda because of the threat that the militias represented and, above all, to see if her family was still alive. Today we know that her whole family was slaughtered during the genocide. Only Rose is still alive.

Alice doesn't exactly remember the presence of militiamen or soldiers in your group. But there were some, weren't there?

Yes, the FAR accompanied us in our flight. We didn't see them much because they led the way and headed us in the right direction. They usually lived with their families in the camps. Some of them no longer had weapons nor even wore their uniforms. Those who had maintained their military roles in the FAR organized themselves to try to cover our escape as best they could. When the RPF soldiers arrived and attacked the camps, the members of the FAR stayed together as a group to try to draw the attention of the RPF and hold them back as long as possible, which allowed us to get a good lead during the first attack.

Once they figured this out, the RPF and their allies (Laurent-Désiré Kabila's* soldiers) grew increasingly inventive in order to surprise the FAR. The second attack took place at night and proved to be much more deadly. The FAR knew that an attack was imminent: we had seen them discussing it and trying to prepare, but they didn't expect the attack to occur that night. Nonetheless, they enabled some of us to escape. During the raid, I was too busy trying to flee with my children amid the widespread panic and didn't see the fighting between the FAR and our attackers.

By the third raid, in Mbandaka, few armed FAR members remained. They were attacked from the rear. Our assailants skirted the camp in order to wedge us against the forest and avoid having to fight directly with the FAR members who were still there.

The militiamen—who had perpetuated the genocide—were also in the camps. They'd fled with everyone. They didn't wear a uniform that let us tell them apart from the other refugees, but from time to time we came across someone who we knew had taken part in the killings.

Some militiamen continued to try to find and kill the Tutsis hidden among the refugees. But there were so many people there that we never dealt with them directly—especially as the health care situation and the flight of the RPF troops quickly become everyone's primary concerns, including those who had been part of the genocide.

Could you tell us about your personal experience of the attack that separated you from your two daughters, as well as the long period of waiting before being reunited with them in Belgium?

We were attacked once again when we were in Mbandaka. It was more violent than the other times. I can say that my true ordeal began then, because we all got separated. People were killed and trampled on; some fell into the river. I ran towards the forest by myself but stopped to call for my children. The people around me didn't want me to cry out, in order to avoid attracting attention to us. I was knocked over by others who were fleeing. I fell down but then got right back up to keep calling for my children. I searched for them for at least three hours while continuing to move forward, but they were nowhere to be found.

I stopped, telling myself that they couldn't be ahead of me. So I started to walk back in the direction of the shooting. The people I passed told me I was crazy and to not go back. I didn't care. I had to keep looking for my children or else they would die behind me.

Luckily for me, the attackers kept chasing people in the forest. So I found myself behind them, where there was no longer any shooting. I was continuing to call for my children when I heard a tiny little voice answer, "Mama, Mama, I'm here!"

It was Aline! She was still sick, but she nonetheless had had the strength to hide herself in the foliage. I took her in my arms and felt mixed relief. I said to myself, "that's one already. Maybe the others aren't far!" I searched for Alice

*The future president of the Democratic Republic of Congo (1997-2001), he led the People's Revolutionary Party and was head of the rebellion in the eastern part of the country as well as being a gold and ivory dealer.

and Adeline in vain until nightfall. We spent the night hidden in the forest. The shots ceased little by little. Some Zairians started coming back to collect things that the refugees had left behind.

After several days of searching in the jungle, I found myself in a small group of about twenty Rwandans who hadn't managed to escape very far. They were either accompanying children who were sick or very young, or were sick themselves. I was still carrying Aline on my back, but I hadn't found my two other daughters, Alice and Adeline.

Some Zairians found us and told us they would show us the way out of the area so that we could get beyond the reach of the soldiers. They didn't trust our attackers (RPF soldiers), who had allied themselves with Laurent-Désiré Kabila's soldiers so as to track us. The Zairians told us they were certain the soldiers were preparing to come back and search the area to ensure that no survivors remained. I very reluctantly had to abandon my search for my missing daughters in order to survive with my daughter Aline. But as I walked, I felt like a zombie. The further I got from that place, the more I had the feeling that I would never see Alice and Adeline again. Yet despite everything, deep down I kept hoping my daughters were still alive and that they might perhaps have been taken in by Zairians.

Going from village to village, we walked to Congo-Brazzaville, where we stayed hidden. Then I continued my journey to meet up with my husband, who was in the Central African Republic. I should have been happy to have gotten out alive but I was still worried and angry. There was little chance that Alice and Adeline had survived, and it made me afraid that I hadn't been able to say goodbye to them one last time, nor to have been able to be with them in their final moments. I imagined their suffering; I imagined they might have died of hunger, from being shot, or even worse.

Other Rwandans began to come alive again, but not me. I didn't open my mouth to talk about what had happened; I stayed stuck in the event during which I'd lost my two daughters. I became depressed.

A tiny hope remained that they were still alive. That's why I kept inquiring and looking. For example, we followed the situation every day on BBC. That's how we learned that some Rwandan refugees still in Zaire had been repatriated to Rwanda. So I wrote a letter and sent it to the village where we'd been living during the war, to find out if anyone from my family had returned and if they knew what had become of my daughters. That was in 1998.

Time passed without my receiving news from anyone. We had two more children. And it was two years after I wrote that letter, during the month of February, 2000, a few months after the birth of the second child, that I received a letter from my sister Médiatrice.

For the rest of my life, I will remember the letter that told me Alice and Adeline were alive and with her. I stopped right in my tracks: I almost fainted. I felt as if I were dreaming. I learned later on that it had taken a miracle for that letter to arrive. My sisters had already written me several times without their letters ever reaching me. Only this one, sent six months earlier, arrived at its destination. I read that letter again and again.

Unfortunately I couldn't communicate by phone or internet. At that time, there was nothing like that available. I wrote back to them—in vain. It was only when I moved to Belgium that I was finally able to hear their voices. For me, that was a miracle. It took a long time to bring them here because Rwanda didn't want to let local residents leave the country. The new Rwandan government wanted expatriated Rwandans to go back to live in their country of origin. It took a long time, but we finally managed to arrange for them to get to Belgium from Kenya.

I think that sometimes miracles happen right in the midst of dramatic events. To this day, I think that finding my daughters still alive was a miracle—and I'll believe that to the end of my life.

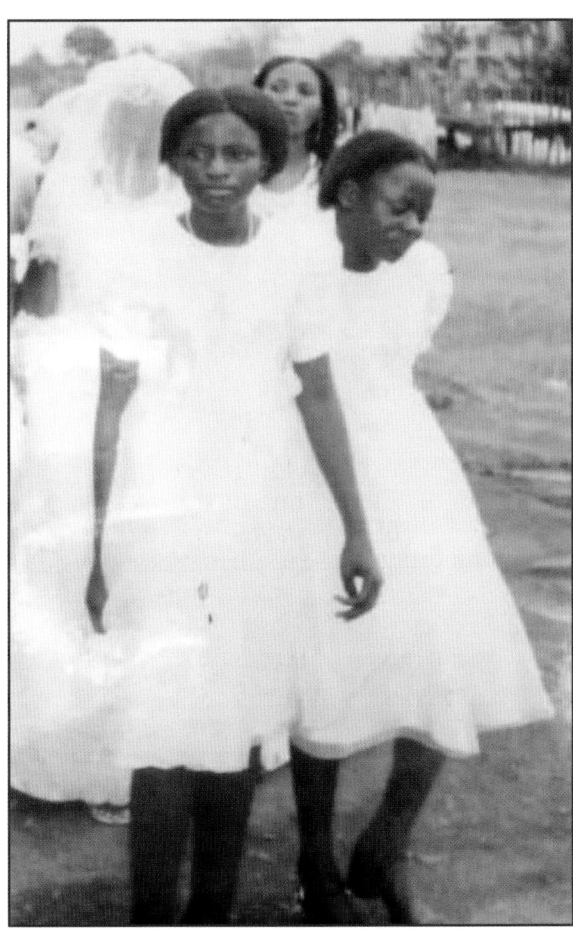

Alice and Adeline. Photo taken in Kenya in 2003, the year of their departure.

Study sketches by the author for Alice's parents

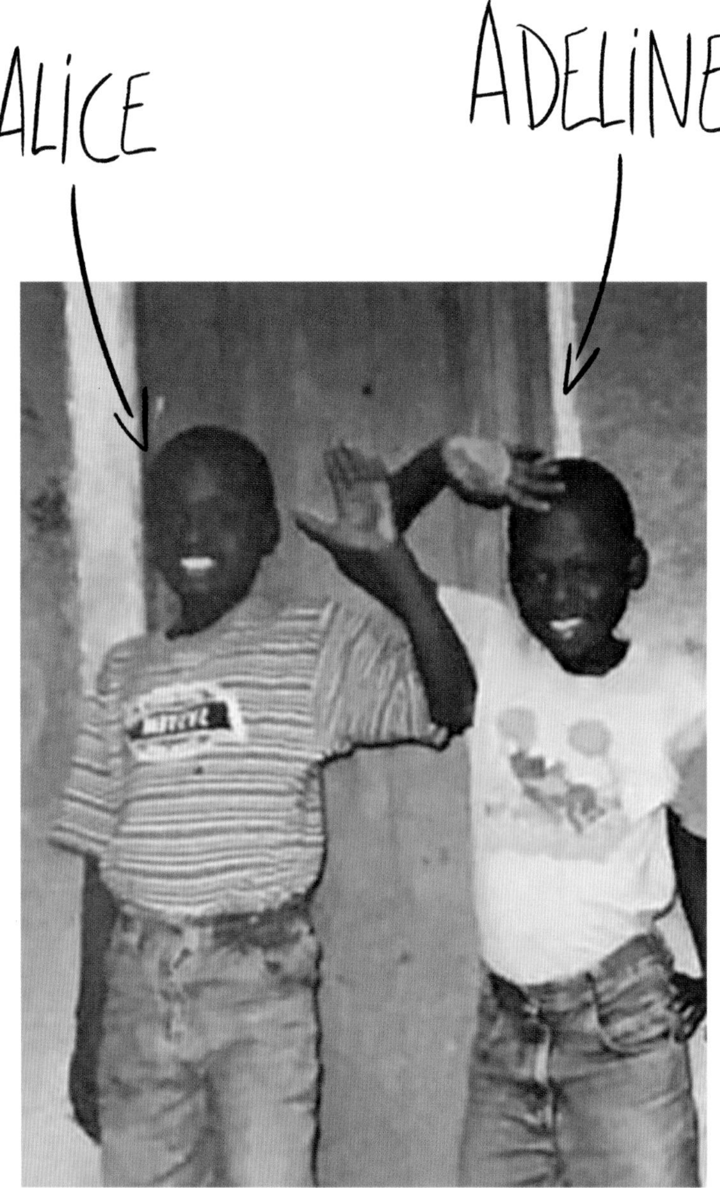

Photo taken in Kenya in 2002, about a year before the two sisters left.

Alice, thank you for having entrusted me with carrying out this project that we care so much about. Thank you also for your patience and for your presence at my side.

Thank you to Vincent Henry as well as to all the members of La Boîte à Bulles for their trust, work, and commitment to this graphic novel.

Gaspard Talmasse